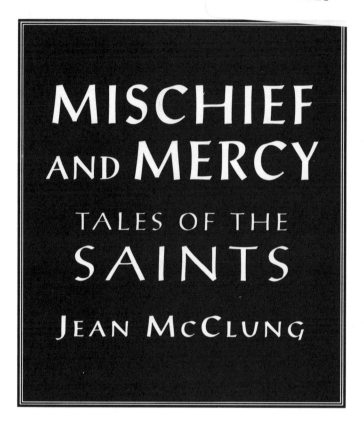

MISCHIEF
AND MERCY
TALES OF THE
SAINTS

Jean McClung

TRICYCLE PRESS
BERKELEY, CALIFORNIA

TRICYCLE PRESS
P.O. Box 7123
Berkeley, CA 94707

Book and cover design by Nancy Austin

"Saint Nicholas of Myra" was originally published
in *Desert Call,* 1990, vol. 25, no. 4.

"The Legend of Saint Dymphna" originally appeared
in *Sexual Abuse: Incest Victims and Their Families,*
J. Goodwin, Wright-PSG, 1982.

Library of Congress Cataloging-in-Publication Data

McClung, Jean, 1946–
Mischief and mercy : tales of the saints / Jean McClung.
p. cm.
Summary: A collection of twelve stories based on the lives of saints and saintly figures, including Francis of Assisi, Joan of Arc, and Valentine.
ISBN 1-883672-02-3
1. Christian saints—Fiction. [1. Saints—Fiction. 2. Short stories.] I. Title.
PS3557.0622M57 1993

813'.54—dc20	93-2487
[E]	CIP
	AC

Manufactured in the United States of America
1 2 3 4 5 – 97 96 95 94 93

For Jim, Amanda, Robert, Paul, and Elizabeth,
whose days may be found here,
and for the cousins

Saints organize time for us not only by connecting us with history but also by sprinkling the year with special days. The underlined days and names you will find in the titles of these tales. You may decide to read a story on or around the day it celebrates. The other days and names are hidden inside the stories and will light up for you only after you read about them.

I know the unspeakable artifice and cleverness of this reverend father...there is no mischief he will not attempt if exasperated.

> (Junípero Serra, as described by one
> of his military colleagues)

Leave me, brother, to rejoice in the Lord and in His praises and in my infirmities, for...I am so united and wedded to my Lord that by His mercy I can well be merry in the Most High.

> —FRANCIS OF ASSISI, on his deathbed,
> when reproved for singing

for Hudson William Charin Struck, on the occasion of his birth, June 4, 2000

Jean McClung Goodwin

WARNING TO THE UNWARY READER

BECAUSE THEY ARE NEITHER TYPICAL nor average, saints, in and of themselves, are rather shocking, as is the evil that attracts itself to their vicinities by some mysterious mystical principle of opposites. The stories in this book have about as much violence as old-fashioned (Brothers Grimm–type) fairy tales, which means there is some chopping up, and about as much sex as the average Greek tragedy, which is a lot. Children should use judgment when reading these stories to grown-ups. They may have to leave out some of the historical bits at the beginning and end of chapters. I have tried my best to clean up the stories themselves but getting the sex and violence out of history is beyond my powers. People more sensitive and squeamish than I tell me there are truly gross quantities of sex and violence in the Mary Magdalene and Joan of Arc stories and that many of the others are nearly as bad, but if I tell you all the names, you will just go read them first.

CONTENTS

"In sum," said Tarrou with simplicity, "what interests me is to know how one becomes a saint."

"But you don't believe in God."

"Exactly. Can one be a saint without God? It is the only concrete modern problem that I know of."

"Perhaps," answered the doctor, "but, you know, I feel more solidarity with the vanquished than the saints. I believe I lack the taste for heroism and sanctity. What interests me is how to be a man."

"Yes, we are searching for the same thing, but I am less ambitious."

—ALBERT CAMUS, *La Peste*

INTRODUCTION

THE STORIES IN THIS BOOK were made for Christmas and for reading out loud and for remembering our own saints by.

Everybody has special memories about Christmas, memories that shine so brightly that we forget that they only lasted for a moment. I think of the moment when I first saw Joe Light's Christmas tree. Joe Light was a real Texas cowboy who lived far away from everything in a shack that was easily accessible only by buggy. We had come out in the pickup with some difficulty. His Christmas tree was a stubby, leafbare mesquite tree that he had dug out with some of its dirt and wedged into a coffee can.

You may not even know what a mesquite looks like; nowadays airplane-sprayed herbicides have made them nearly extinct. Mesquites are gigantic thorn trees that thrive in the drought-prone great plains. At least, they used to thrive. The wonder of this mesquite was that you could pin whatever you wanted onto it by its thorns—a Christmas card or a chocolate-covered cherry or a dollar. You could hang things on the thorns, too—a bottle opener or a fingernail clipper or a Boy Scout whistle or one of those blue speckled tin spoons with a hole in the handle. It's true that this image only stayed perfect for about a minute before all the surrounding realities set in: the waves of heat from the wood stove, and the smell of Joe's spit can, and the fact that once again I hadn't figured out what to say to Joe Light. But none of that dims it, and there is another good part to that memory which has to do with reading at Christmas, because Joe Light found for me a wonderful old book of Texas heroes which I read straight through that night by the oil lamp in lieu of trying to find my

1

bearings in the conversation. It was an old school book that looked as though it had seen a lot of use right around the turn of the century. There were chapters on the pirate Jean Laffitte and chapters about Travis and Bowie. One or the other of those guys might have been a saint, I guess. They caused enough damage. Jean Laffitte was one of those annoying people like King Arthur who did not have the good grace to breathe his last in full view of an official historian, so there is always the suspicion that he could still be out there somewhere pirating away, maybe working for Andy Jackson on the side.

Visiting the Alamo, where Travis and Bowie died, was probably my first pilgrimage. As a teenager, though, it never occurred to me that saints might be what those doomed rebels were and that pilgrimage is what we have to keep doing with such people. A lot of those guys who died at the Alamo had come to Texas on the run, and I guess they had just got real tired of running. Travis had left Alabama in an awful hurry. They say he found his wife in bed with another man. Some say he killed the man. Others say he didn't and the not killing him was what Travis was running from. Bowie was too much of wreck to run. He had filled his youth with every indulgence, vice, and adventure his society knew: slave-trading, pirating, land speculation, duels. He was enormously popular. They say he rode alligators down the bayous and that his horse was shod with silver from his secret lost mine. He made fortunes and lost fortunes. Then he converted to Catholicism and married the love of his life, a Spanish lady, and then the cholera came and carried her off and his children and her parents, his entire reconstructed family, and he had been drunk ever since. It was at the Alamo that Bowie found a way to use what was left of his life. They say his dead body was found surrounded by piles of Santa Ana's soldiers. Unable to get up from his sick bed, he'd laid into them with his famous knife.

Joe Light may have been a saint, too. At least I know it was extra nice of him to find me that good book that night.

I may have been interested in saints even before Joe Light and the Alamo because of my Aunt Ima. She was like those people Auden talks about in his poem on Freud's death: "They die among us every day, those who were trying to do us some good and knew it was never enough but hoped to improve a little by living." She was always cooking stuff for people and going to the hospital to see somebody sick and sewing mattresses for migrants sleeping on shack floors or monkey dolls for children stuck in the hospital. I never realized until I was grownup how difficult it is to do good. Most of us mess it up when we try and then we stop trying. But I think my Aunt Ima must have gone about it just the right way, because she always gave things to me in a way that worked. She'd turn up to up to play dominos on a winter night when I was so sick I was ready to die. Or she'd take me out and buy me a black sundress with bright pink flowers on a day when I was feeling too evil and ugly even to look at myself. She was also really funny and absolutely loved all the things about this world and the way it's put together and the crazy way that humans act. I'm thinking about her in her bonnet, weeding a garden that had to be big enough to feed two counties. I'm seeing how she would drape a sheet over the card table so we kids would have a place to hide. She knew about children and how we always need hideouts, as many hideouts as we can find, down in the cellar or up in the mulberry tree or out in the hayloft.

Mostly I hid out with books. When I was about ten somebody (maybe it was Aunt Ima) ordered for us, out of the Neiman-Marcus catalogue, a book of Hans Christian Anderson stories that came in a pretty box with this wonderful candle. The candle had a line marked on it for each of the twenty-four days before Christmas. I know now that these candles come from Scandinavia but back then I had no idea that they were part of anyone else's culture. It was like Neiman-Marcus had imported that one candle straight from God, into the wilds of North Texas just because they'd heard there was somebody out there who especially needed such an object. At least that was the way it felt listening to those stories and watching His candle burn down a little lower each night.

That book was where I discovered *The Little Matchgirl.* Later we read *The Nutcracker* at Christmas and, in high school, Charles Dickens's *A Christmas Carol,* and, in college, Dylan Thomas's *A Child's Christmas in Wales.* With my own children I've added Isaac Bashevis Singer's *The Extinguished Lights* and Truman Capote's *A Christmas Memory.*

The twelve stories here could be read with one of those Scandinavian candles, half a story each night, on the twenty-four December nights before Christmas morning. Or, you might choose to save them for the twelve bleaker days of Christmas between December 25 and Epiphany when the anticipation has died out with the dying year and an icy and merciless winter has set in.

I've arranged the twelve saints in chronological order, starting with the ones who knew Jesus and ending with the ones like Jean Vianney who were alive at the same time as Travis and Bowie. One of my kinfolk knew Travis and Bowie, a great-great-grandfather whose granddaughter, my great-grandmother, was still alive when I was born. It felt good to order the saints that way because it is like a family with each generation echoing and then going on from the ones that went before and all of them making somehow a human bridge that is stronger than time.

The stories themselves were not written in that order. I wrote one a year for twelve years as a Christmas present for family and friends. To have put them in the order in which they were written would reveal too much about me and how I grew in those twelve years. Some of the saints were picked because their day (with saints it's the deathday that's important) coincides with the birthdate of a child I love. Amadour, Robert Southwell, Paul the Simple, and Lazarus entered the book in this apparently random way. Some of the saints I encountered on pilgrimage—Dymphna in Geel, Belgium; Francis in Assisi, Italy; Bluebeard's daughter in Notre Dame cathedral in Paris; Junípero in Carmel, California. One of my all-time peak experiences was being handed, in the British Museum Library, a copy of a book that Robert Southwell had written while in hiding and had printed on the secret Jesuit press in London in 1595. Robertson Davies's book *Fifth Business* is the best modern explanation I know of the joys of such pilgrimages.

As Boris Pasternak said, it is not easy to live one's life, not the same thing at all as to walk across a field. So saints became useful as examples of how to do this indescribable thing. More than that, saints offer us the opportunity to admire them, and there is something enormously healing about admiration. It scours clean the layers of cynicism, criticism, and character assassination that corrode much of our media-dominated lives. My pilgrimages include my own modern saints—Frank Lloyd Wright, Jan Yoors, Ernie Pyle, Jean Moulin, Frida Kahlo, Aldo Leopold, Elvin Semrad. I leave it to you to track down my modern saints and others from your own experience. If you did find some of mine and a few of your own, and if you wrote just one children's story each year about one of them, in a mere twelve years...

JESUS
AND HIS
FOLLOWERS

MARY MAGDALENE

AND DID THOSE FEET
IN ANCIENT TIMES

...and all the earth was made joyful because her womb
brought forth corn and because the birds
of the firmament built their nests in her.

—SAINT HILDEGARDE

MARY MAGDALENE

I ALWAYS THINK OF MARY MAGDALENE as a kind of antidote to
Mary the Virgin, the sorrowful and holy Mother of God. As holy as
Mary is, that is how profane the Magdalene can be. As ultimate a
virgin as Mary is, that is the measure of the Magdalene's harlotry.
Mary is a sorrowing mother pinioned by her love; the Magdalene is
free and footloose, following Christ and her inclinations wherever
they may lead. Mary packs Christ away into His tomb; the Magdalene
turns from her weeping to find Him alive for her again. Mary is
always there to watch Christ suffer; the Magdalene makes Him laugh.
Mary is borne down by the weight of His murdered body; the
Magdalene caresses His living thirsty feet with her long hair. Mary
bears up bravely beneath the burden of her sorrows; the Magdalene
weeps, pitches hysterical fits, and collapses at the foot of the cross,
clutching passionately at those pierced feet that she adores.

An antidote and an embarrassment. From the beginning to the
end Mary Magdalene was an embarrassment. The Pharisees were
embarrassed that such a creature would even be allowed into the
prophet's entourage. Martha was mortally offended that the
Magdalene never helped around the house. Not only that, but she
couldn't be made to feel guilty about it. Judas was offended that she
wasted money, and even worse that she wasted it on luxuries and
sensual delights. Everyone was embarrassed that she was mentally
ill, possessed of seven devils, and everyone was more than a little
unnerved that she was so sexy.

Sources of embarrassment crescendo once we leave the gospels
and enter the forests of folklore. Folktales tell us that she had been in

fact a "good girl" until Saint John the Evangelist jilted her to become an apostle. Her rage and spite and thwarted passion then drove her to bury herself in every imaginable indulgence and aberration (the reader may pause here to imagine an indulgence or aberration of their choice). D. H. Lawrence and others before him have speculated, on the basis I believe of accurate insights into the Magdalene's character, that, when Christ told her on the first Easter morning *"noli me tangere"* ("don't touch me"), she did not obey. Instead, she embraced him with that rapturous pent-up agony of passion which she more than any other woman embodies. Some say that the offspring of this rapture went on to produce the Merovingian royal house of France. Thus France's kings, so they say, are of the corporeal as well as spiritual lineage of Christ. Even so it seems somehow a shame that the Magdalene should be reduced by any means, however fateful and regal, to being merely barefoot and pregnant.

France is the source of most of the other outrageous legends about the Magdalene as well. The French, I suppose, have the only culture human enough to contain and comprehend her; they seem to bear embarrassment better than the English-speaking world. They don't seem to mind so much about her breasts and all that. I suppose the French would call her a *femme femme,* their highest type of woman, a woman who is a woman. She is often portrayed stark naked and reading a book in La Sainte Baume, the hermit's cave where she lived for thirty years and where the birds brought her the Host (a legend used to support the movement to allow women into priesthood. You see what I mean about her being an embarrassment.) Strange pilgrimages are made to this cave. Young girls bury their left garters secretly there and then, at their next fertile time of the moon, build small castles out of pebbles with a large, long phallic sort of pebble in the center...but perhaps this is embarrassing you?

The story I will tell about Mary Magdalene is not as racy as most. It is based on one of the French legends about how she healed a child shortly after she and her companions landed at Marseilles. All the hagiographers (those people who study and know saints) seem so definite in their assertions that these primitive French legends are based on inadequate investigation that I have given one of them the chance to interrogate a key witness in the case. I have also given Mary Magdalene Multiple Personality Disorder. This is based in part on a seventeenth-century painting by Livio Mehus which shows seven of her—a nun, a harlot, a hermit, and (depicted faintly in the background) four cherubic children.

AND DID THOSE FEET
IN ANCIENT TIMES

Certain? Nothing in all this is certain. I don't think you understand. Let me begin again. What I really remember is the rain. There was a rain, nothing but rain all that summer. I was little—eight, maybe nine. We spoke to each other in Latin, which none of us knew very well. I was out of my mind with fever. All I know for certain are the names. I learned their names because they stayed in my room. Mary Magdalene, Lazarus, Martha.

Yes, I can understand how you would assume that my parents would remember. Even I assumed that briefly, and I have known them more than thirty years. But actually my mother showed the strangers into my room that day long ago because she thought it was empty. She'd forgotten about me. My parents don't even remember that I was ill. At least, they say they don't remember. I was so ill. My thoughts got so heavy. My legs got so heavy they wouldn't move at all. Then my chest got heavy. I couldn't make it lift up to let the air in. I was dying.

My parents fought bitterly enough at the time about my being sick. That was why I thought they might remember. She blamed him because he had taken me hunting and I had gotten cut off from the rest and lost in the rain. It was hours before they found me treed by a boar, and I was ill already when they came. He was angry because she left me alone in that room in the tower. She was having an affair with the centurion,

Marcus, so I was used to her going away all the time but when I woke and was paralyzed, I got scared.

That's when I noticed the strangers on the road. I latched onto them with such a terrible intensity, because watching them made me not alone. At first I though Marcus was going to kill all three of them. I could see his arrow ready in the guard tower next to mine, pointing steadily through the narrow window slit. And I could see the strangers blue and white through my own window, winding up the path to our fort. "Don't," I cried. It came out loud, and the arrow moved away. It was as if something inside me had mustered all my remaining strength and lucidity and fastened it onto those three wandering shapes. All my perceptions of them remained untouched by the fever, unshakably clear. Perhaps that was what you meant about being certain? I knew for certain they had come by sea, from far away. I knew they must be seeking the rulers of this country, perhaps to make some request. That's why they had chosen to trudge up the great hill to our fortress. Perhaps Marcus knew all this as well and that was why he stayed his hand. Perhaps he never heard my shout. Perhaps it wasn't even Marcus at the bow but one of the other Romans. Perhaps it was all just a dream.

Mary Magdalene is the one I remember most and the one I can least describe. She sat by my pallet day and night and told me stories while Martha brought broth and cold cloths and Lazarus looked out the window at the sky. Lazarus was an incredible person. He was always finding a patch of sky to gaze at, as if he was looking into the face of a sleeping friend at the point of waking, as if the sky were just about to speak to him and tell him all the secrets of life. I remember one day we lost him the dungeons. We went back and there he was transfixed before a tiny chink in the stone; he'd found the one spot of sky in that maze of darkness.

I remember the stories, but I get mixed up when I try to describe how she looked. Sometimes I thought she was a boy my age. At other times she seemed like an old man in a cave wound around with a long white beard.

The stories? They were about a lot of different people—a little boy and an old hermit, a prostitute, a priestess, a young woman of good family, two even smaller children. They were all waiting—waiting and waiting for so long that each one finally gave up on everything they had dreamed. Each one came to realize that it had gotten too late. But they all kept searching a little bit anyway, even though in their hearts they knew it was no use. That was when, one by one, they found this man Jesus, and everything changed.

That was the plot, but one day she said a strange thing, one of those things I didn't know how to think about, except to remember it. She said, "And once we found Him and knew Him, we knew each other as well and knew in fact that we had known each other forever and finally that all of us were one." At first I thought that was Christian philosophy or something, but now I think she meant it literally—that these were all different spirits living in her body and that when this Jesus knew each of them and each of them knew Him that they got to know each other and the knowing made her no longer possessed.

Yes, I would say it was seven spirits, the same as the number of characters in the story. Is that important?

The way the story went, each of the seven found Jesus in a different way. The boy was working on a fishing boat that Jesus hired, and the boy decided he had never seen anyone so funny and so graceful and so brave. The old hermit was living in a cell in the desert when Jesus came to visit another hermit in that colony. No, I don't remember the names of those other hermits. Maybe a John? The names weren't important, just that he had felt so alone before, so cut off from God, and was healed by this Jesus.

Now where was I? It was even more complicated to follow that first day when I was so sick, but in a way I liked that because

I lost myself in it. I felt better lost. The prostitute saw Jesus in the streets and fell in love with His body—His eyes, the way He grinned, the look of His back as he walked. The rich young woman heard Him preaching in some temple and became His student. The priestess worked in the temple with His mother and learned prophecies and saw omens and read stars that made her decide Jesus was the fulfillment of all these things. The little ones were begging on the road and He let them come with them and gave them food and water.

Martha? She and Mary Magdalene fought a lot. Mary Magdalene had this alabaster bottle of medicine that she kept around her neck and Martha kept telling her that she had better not use it on me. "Don't be a fool and waste it on that one. He's already dead," Martha said. She thought I was asleep, but I wasn't. It didn't scare me anyway because that's what I thought, too. Martha said that Mary Magdalene had saved it a long time, ever since Jesus died, and she should keep saving it for Lazarus because he was delicate.

That was the first I knew of Jesus being dead because Mary Magdalene spoke as if He were alive. And I hadn't thought of Lazarus as delicate either. His hair was all white, his eyebrows and even the hair on his chest and stomach and legs was white, but his face was like a baby's, and sleeping with him was like sleeping with a baby. He felt warm and soft and smelled sweet.

I loved being near of all their bodies those first days when I was sick. Mary Magdalene's breasts were the first I'd ever noticed. They're all I can sense when I try to see her in my mind's eye. It was like her breasts were everything she was. They were like flowers at their peak, like twin rainbows reminding us how God keeps His hand upon us humans. For they were so made that God must have molded them with His own hand, and once they were made, how could God have kept His hands off...

No, I guess I don't have much more to say about the breasts of Mary Magdalene. I'm sorry if I offended. You don't want to hear about Martha's body, either? I thought you people were serious about trying to identify them. All I wanted to say is that I loved to be touched by those three. I hadn't been touched at all in such a long, long time, and I was ill, and I missed them like fire when they left.

Did Mary Magdalene use the medicine from the bottle on me after all? That's an interesting question. You must decide if the answer is yes or no. She told me one night that Martha was being foolish because the medicine had all been used up a long time ago anyway. It was rare stuff called spikenard from even futher east than their home, and there was no way to replace it. For years now the bottle had held only water, but she was too intimidated by Martha and the rest to explain that. She had been planning to use the medicine to wash Jesus' body after He was dead. Or maybe that was Martha's plan. Who could remember after all these years?

She turned her head away from me a little with this sly smile. "I've never told anyone the real story. I always say that because the body wasn't there I never needed to use the rest of the spikenard. But that morning when I went to the tomb, already there was water in the bottle, only water."

"So what had you done with the medicine?" I asked.

"I washed my hair with it," she said, and then she laughed and laughed, and I saw she was crying too. "I felt so awful that night He died. It had been a terrible day and a terrible night before that and all I could feel was black misery, and what terrified me most was knowing I was going to fall apart again. I had used the first part of the stuff in the bottle to wash His feet. Everyone else hated that but I knew and He knew it was right. Really right. And it didn't feel right at all to use the rest on His dead body. It seemed even less right when Martha said it would be just fine. Martha's always been a kind of moral bellwether for me. Whatever she recommends I know I should worry about. I don't know how to explain...I couldn't sleep and I felt like I was dying so I washed my hair."

And now she was laughing again, and we both laughed and she filled the bottle up with water and poured it over my head and it was wonderful. Just like she said, it made me feel better, wonderfully better. As it happened, at that moment, the paralysis went away and the fever left me and I could breathe, but it wasn't really the healing part that felt so good. Old Lazarus woke up as we were laughing, and he looked at both of us for a long time as if trying to figure us out and then he exclaimed all of a sudden, "God is love" with great conviction as if that explained everything perfectly, and then he went to the narrow window and gazed out at the sky. Actually, I never heard Lazarus say anything else. Every time you asked him a question, Lazarus would think about it for a long, long time and finally answer, with the happiness of one who has at last found the perfect solution, "God is love."

I can't believe that's what people say. That my parents converted the whole kingdom to Christianity because Mary Magdalene healed me with this magic stuff? What rot. Well, as I've already told you, there was no magic stuff. And my parents didn't seem to know for sure if I was dead or alive, much less sick or well. It's not that I don't love them. I love my parents all the time. It's just that I can't stand them. They affect me like an illness. I can feel the paralysis gradually taking hold. What a mixed-up idea, though, that my parents converted the kingdom. See, Mary Magdalene never inhabited my father's kingdom at all. And my father's kingdom is still there, just as lonely and meaningless as ever. I wake up in it some mornings as if trapped in a bad dream. Kings can't get you into that kingdom where Mary Magdalene lived. Kings don't do religion. They do wars and hunts and feasts and love affairs and the making and breaking of promises.

I'm not even certain that I do religion. Whatever it is that I do, my parents don't interfere. Maybe that counts for something. Call it converting the kingdom if you wish.

What I try to do is remember...which is very painful because

I miss those three so much. I miss everything about them. Most of all I miss the ordinariness of them. They were just people. They were foolish, they argued. Mary Magdalene would say Jesus talked about love, not money, and Martha would say He did so talk about money, and then she told this funny story about someone hiring workers for a vineyard and then Mary Magdalene said she never had liked that one and why didn't Martha just forget it and Lazarus thought that was a question and answered thoughtfully, "God...is...Love," and Mary Magdalene said on second thought why not go tell it to the King and Queen because she certainly had not got through to them with her stories and Lazarus thought was a question too and we were all cozy together under the same blanket except Lazarus crawled out every so often to look at the sky.

I know it doesn't sound like much. They only stayed with me for three days....But it's all I ever had, and if I keep working it right I think it may last me a long, long time.

Maybe forever.

POSTSCRIPT

The day of Saint Lazarus is December 17, which may be the best Christmastime day for reading this story. Another good way to celebrate his day is to look at the sky and say "God is love" one hundred times. Mary Magdalene and Martha are remembered in the middle of summer; on July 22, you might like to pour some champagne over your head (it feels really good) and on July 29 you can clean house in honor of Martha...clean and clean and clean until you are dizzy, rapt and ecstatic.

AMADOUR AND VERONICA

HIS OWN ACCOUNT OF
THE TRUE IMAGE

For in my nature I quested for beauty, but God,
God hath sent me to the sea for pearls.

—CHRISTOPHER SMART, *Jubilate Agno*

The world, somebody wrote,
is the place we prove real by dying in it.

—SALMAN RUSHDI, *The Satanic Verses*

AMADOUR AND VERONICA

Amadour is one of the saints most thoroughly deplored by hagiographers. They have to admit that an incorrupt body was definitely discovered in 1166 at Rocamadour, in France. But to assume that it was the body of the first hermit to dig cells into that rock! To assume that he had been a contemporary of Christ! To imagine that he was the husband of Veronica, the Veronica who wiped Christ's face with her veil as He fell beneath the weight of His cross! To gratuitously identify Amadour with the tax collector Zaccheus who, Luke said, climbed a tree to catch a glimpse of Jesus! This, every iota of this sort of imagining, the hagiographers consider to be a scandalous assault on truth.

All of which make me sad, seeing once again that the things I love don't love each other. For I cannot bring myself to doubt a single one of those assumptions about that incorrupt body. Like all the other knights and crusaders who have made pilgrimages to Rocamadour since the twelfth century and before, I am an absolute sucker for every improbable twist in that most unlikely, and therefore, most plausible legend.

But I love the hagiographers, too. I keep trying to find one particular story about a hagiographer and a tube of blood, but keep losing it among all those other stories of saints and blesseds, so I cannot tell you for sure from which incorrupt Italian saintly relic the blood had been drawn. Nonetheless, the local legend was that the blood would become unclotted on certain holy days, and would flow liquid and alive again. So, this one hagiographer obtained a vial of this dried, ancient, holy blood and carried it with him for days, for months, yes, even for years. He examined the tube at every opportunity, and with utmost scrutiny on holy days. After studying his vial for so many days and so many nights he was able to attest with some certitude that the blood had never once come unclotted. This is the quest of a true hero, someone who must have yearned more than I can imagine to see that blood just once grow warm and bright again and fluid. This is the sort of thing that makes me love hagiographers; but even more, I love to believe, with them but despite them, in the very saints they most deplore.

Veronica is deplored by the hagiographers somewhat less fervently than Amadour. She is identified in some legends as the woman whose issue of blood was healed by Jesus. Some scholars believe this to be an early reference to the hemorrhages caused by tuberculosis. Other versions say she was the wife of a Roman functionary. Her veil is still preserved in Saint Peter's, in Rome, and even the most skeptical of hagiographers is satisfied that it has been there since the early 700s at least. However, by now, no one can discern any image whatsoever on that cloth.

Amadour is remembered on August 20, and Veronica on July 12. Christ was crucified in 30 A.D.; Tiberius died in 37 A.D.; and Peter and Paul were executed during Nero's persecution of the Christians after Rome burned in 64 A.D.

HIS OWN ACCOUNT OF
THE TRUE IMAGE

I Amadour, am writing from the rock where I have lived these seven years. For many months I have wanted to write something of how I came here, and wished many times that I had writing materials. I have had only myself and the rock and the crucifixion nail that I use to shape my cave, nothing more. There are some old statues, too; I had forgotten them.

Today, however, a poet came to me. To be honest, he is only a singing vagabond, wandering for a year in order to write great verse. Truly, I believe, that, in accepting from him this blank scroll, I relieved him of a dreadful burden. The scroll is not, in fact, all together blank, as you can see. The doggerel below, that my script surrounds, is the work of my benefactor.

> Over the mountain, over the sea,
>
> In every fountain, I try to see me.

That was his only effort in what had been more than half a year, by my reckoning. He said that he left in the summer. Now it is the wet end of winter. He slept two nights in my cave. He speaks Latin and was not as afraid of me as the villagers hereabouts. They continue to bring me food because, I think, I terrify them, and they wish to appease me.

It was summer too, long ago, when Veronica and I set out to bring the True Image to Rome. That was a good many wet winters ago, but I remember setting out beneath the summer sun as vividly as any of what followed. That was the summer when we took the names that became our own: Veronica and Amadour, the True Image and the Lover, the Amateur. Before that, we were Susanna and Zaccheus of Jericho. Susanna the ill, frail shadow of herself and Zaccheus the tax collector and lover of Romans. Perhaps if we had fared better as Susanna and Zaccheus we could have remained who they were, living out their lives. However, under their names we were perfect failures.

I was not even a very good tax collector. The others chose me to deal with the Romans because I had the misfortune to love Romans. All the other Jewish tax collectors hated them, you see, and negotiations between Jews and Romans went predictably sour. I had never meant to love the Romans. Indeed I prayed at great length to be spared the love of them that has always been in me. Much of my love has to do with the art they brought, especially the statues (statues mostly stolen, I understand, from Greece, Egypt and Chaldea). Knowing that my Romans had not created those wonderful objects, but had merely pilfered them, never helped me to stop loving Romans. Had Romans not stolen the things, I would not have seen them. Each time I saw a fresco, a painted vase, or a graven image of some tawdry, alleged God, each time, a new heaven and a new earth opened up before me.

I should explain that I was born a Jew and that no images, drawn or sculpted, or human beings or of beasts, were allowed to us. Cruelly, I was also born with the ability to create faithful images of whatever my eyes behold. This curse, which set me at odds with my own people and with our law, I knew as a blessing only because I knew Romans. I had seen the images on their coins, shields, and standards, and I knew they would value what I did.

While my more astute tax-collecting friends argued terms for new contracts, I would sketch the Roman bureaucrat before us. As he became more and more relaxed and reassured in the contemplation of his image, as I fashioned it, my model became remolded into a prime target for our brotherhood of swindlers.

Everyone who was not a Roman despised my gift, even my beloved wife, Susanna. She prayed for me a great deal. She made me bury my drawings and my statues beneath the clay floors of our Grotto. She even believed that my art had caused the illness which made her frail and childless, that, because I created beings in wood, God would not allow her to conceive and grow His image in our own flesh. At times I believed she hated me because my sin had caused her loss.

Jesus of Nazareth was the only Jew who ever accepted me for what I am. He had cured Susanna and she became His follower. That was how I came to know Him. Susanna had the White Sickness for many years. Attacks would make her bleed, and the bleeding made her unclean. In a bleeding attack she was not even allowed to enter the Synagogue to pray for forgiveness for my sins or to ask forgiveness for her own inability to forgive or even to tolerate me.

I have never been sure whether Jesus cured the bleeding itself or whether he cured the bitterness that had grown up around the bleedings, so that with the bitterness gone, the bleeding simply crept away into the background of our lives. Susanna, my Veronica, suffered with the White Sickness until the end of her life, but how can I explain? After Jesus cured her, the Sickness ceased to have any importance for her, or for me, or for the people at the Synagogue. Jesus of Nazareth removed the sickness from her mind, from all of our minds, and that was His cure.

So, she followed Him. She spoke to me always of Jesus, but I never attended to what she said. What fascinated me was the look of the man. Again and again I asked her to describe Him, but all she could tell were contradictions. "He is a man of sorrows." "He is all joy." "He is not a big fellow." "He fills up one's mind. You see no one else." "He is gentle." "He is mighty." I knew that all I needed was a quill, and ten minutes' sight of Him, and this thicket of words would give way to a true image.

So, when I heard that Jesus was coming to Jericho, I found a tall tree that overlooked the road near the Synagogue where

He was certain to come to argue with the Masters. That was what Susanna was full of, the wonderful arguments of Jesus. I was waiting there in the tree, watching for Him when He came. It was tricky business, because I had to hide both my despised tax-collecting person and the fact that I was sketching. It was late Spring, and the leaves of the tree gave me cover. I was using an accounting scroll to draw on. It was all so misguided—my preoccupation, as much as my ruse. Jesus came and looked straight up into the tree at me, laughing. "Come to me, Zaccheus," he said. "I see you today through the eyes of the image of me that you are drawing. I saw you yesterday, as well, when the eyes of my image were only a hope in your mind."

The drawing went wrong, too. Not that it mattered at the time. He came and ate with us. He made me dig my statues out of the floor. He loved seeing them. He knew most of the Roman bureaucrats, too, recognized them in my sketches, and talked of their vagaries and sayings, and their books and faces and houses, as if He were afflicted, like me, with some inescapable love for them.

It is an awesome and painful thing to be appreciated in the way that Jesus appreciated us. The appreciation soaked into me until it reached down to my very bones; then it started soaking into my spirit too, a spirit which turned out to be much larger than I had imagined, with tentacles or toes, or roots, or whatever it is that spirits use to stretch themselves, that reached away up—sometimes as far as the places where God arranges the clouds.

One other thing that happened that day was that Susanna fell in love with me. We had been married for ten years and she had been a good wife. But, after that day, she looked at me with love. Every moment we were together, her eyes sought me out and smiled at me with the greatest pleasure.

It was after He left that the wrongness of the drawing began to bedevil me. In the sketch, He was looking up, happy to recognize me, laughing at me, knowing me, knowing how miserably unhappy and lonely I was, glad to be with me. It was too much. I would finally capture one part of it, but then the rest of it would disappear. I even went to Bethany to try to catch another glimpse of Him. He could not see me, because He was raising someone from the dead, or maybe trying to explain something to his disciples. I forget; you see, none of that was important to me. At the time, only His face mattered to me.

For this reason, I did not see Him crucified. Susanna was there, in Jerusalem. I was in Jericho, sketching Roman bureacrats by day and endlessly revising that uplifted face of Jesus of Nazareth by night. And so, He died, and I was not there to see.

Also, I missed Veronica's miracle. (I will call her Veronica now rather than Susanna, because it was at this time, when Jesus died, that I, in my mind, began calling her by that name.) Veronica was one of those people who always live near miracles; I live in the opposite direction, in the neighborhood of work, far from those places where miracles are made.

I have sometimes felt, though, that there might be a path between my lonely neighborhood and Veronica's. There have been moments when I have given myself up to the work so entirely and without question that it seemed if I kept on long enough, I might come around to a miracle, too, at the end. Even that second, most famous miracle for Veronica may have been intended for me, a little, as well. Certainly, I never would have completed the statue of Jesus without it.

Let me tell you what happened. Jesus had been condemned, scourged by the Roman lash, mocked, and crowned with thorns, and was carrying the cross-piece for His crucifixion to Calvary. The vertical piece they reused; it was erected already on the hill. Veronica, in that compulsively helpful way that she has, ran up to Him as He staggered under His cross, and, as he looked up in her face, she tenderly wiped the blood from His eyes with her veil. That was all. She came home to me the next day, too tired and ill even to put herself to bed. I removed her veil, and saw on it the elusive image of Jesus that I had been struggling to capture for weeks.

No one else ever saw it immediately in the way that I could. Veronica worked for days to learn how to see it straight off each time. The image was faint, with the light where the darkness should have been, and the two halves of the face were reversed, I think.

So I completed my sketch, and after that, a statue, though neither one ever pleased me entirely. Also, we became the custodians of a Treasure. After Pentecost, many pilgrims came to see the image. It was always the same. They would look first at the veil, with growing boredom and incomprehension. I would try to teach them to see what was there. At last, when all of us were thoroughly frustrated and disappointed, I would take them to the courtyard to see the statue, at which they could finally and honestly gasp. Veronica always told the story of the True Image, because she believed that listening to the story was the only way for ordinary people to see it. She told them that it was because she had tried to live in the image of Jesus by reaching out lovingly to help that the image of Jesus had remained with her.

During those years, we were often an embarrassment to the Christian synagogue in Jerusalem. I, a tax-collector, was a less-than-devout Jew, to put it mildly. And Veronica was neither predictably nor ordinarily devout, with her frequent illnesses and solitary meditations. Yet, because of the treasured image, the Jerusalem Christians were forced to include us. I have always believed that God was answering not only my prayers but also the prayers of all the devout Jews in our group when he found a way to get Veronica and me out of Jerusalem and away to Rome.

In order to answer our prayers, God, it seemed, had needed to go directly to the top, for it took a personal command from Tiberius Caesar that the True Image of Christ be brought to him at Capri, where he lay ill. At that time we had grown accustomed to understanding that when people asked to see the true image, that what they truly wanted to see was the false image, that is, my execrable statue. However, Veronica and I thought it possible that someone like Caesar might mean exactly what he said, so we ended up bringing both the statue and the veil.

As it turned out, Caesar wanted neither one; he was only looking for a little magic. How vividly I remember coming into his room, because I wanted immediately to paint all of it. Out the windows, you could see the rest of the island and the blue sea beyond. He was an ill old man, shivering and miserable with fever, but powerful still and utterly Roman. He liked my statue and kept it for his own. I was grateful to be robbed of it because that day I saw nothing in it but utterly misguided error and failure. Veronica had worn the veil so we would have it in case of need, but camouflaged, so that, unless absolutely necessary, we would not have to risk our heads by trying to persuade Caesar to see the nearly invisible image on the cloth. He lay there, touching his new statue, shaking with chills and sweating with fever, and Veronica reached over with her veil to wipe the drops of sweat from his forehead.

It is a crime to touch the Caesar, but no one noticed such things with Veronica. Also, at the touch of her veil, Tiberius Caesar was cured. This stunned all of us so much that orderly thinking stopped. Later, Veronica would tell the story of this new miracle in this way: If you dare to break the rules and touch someone with loving help, good things are bound to happen, no matter how grim it looks at first.

For a long time after that miracle, no good things happened that I could see. Tiberius was one of those people who react to good luck by becoming enraged that it had not come earlier. He began an investigation into why Christ's True Image had not been prescribed for him years before. Tiberius had suffered attacks of the Roman swamp fever since his first campaign with the Legions. At last, the palace lackeys seized on Pontius Pilate as a credible culprit. Pilate had misjudged the Man and had Him crucified, they said. Otherwise Jesus would be available at this very moment to serve Caesar's every whim. So Pilate and his wife Claudia, a Christian, though, not a Jew, were first exiled from Jerusalem and then executed near a river called the Danube.

Tiberius made plans to return from Capri to Rome so as to regain active control of the government. However, his relatives poisoned him while he was on the journey. The amnesty for Christians that Tiberius had promised was never honored by any of his revolting successors.

Somehow, though, the two of us got off that island and safely back to Rome. Veronica asked the church at Rome to take over the veil for safekeeping. I found a room for us above one of the city gates near a carpenter for whom I did some woodwork. We settled down to live, but I kept thinking about that miracle.

"Who benefited from it? Caligula? Caligula's many victims?" I used to ask Veronica. "Surely not the murdered Tiberius or our executed friend Claudia?" Veronica always answered, "Maybe it is we two who were blessed."

We had been relieved of those perplexing images, both the true and the false. I was free now to carve statues, statues which all Rome wanted to buy. Veronica could be with me, watching all day as I worked. In the Roman church, for the first time, we were accepted by other Christians. I spend my days loving Romans; Veronica spent hers loving me; and more and more friends came to love us and the images I made. It was as though we were finally free to be, on the outside, the people that we had been always secretly within. It was in this way that Veronica and I began to grow old.

There remained one corner of my life which continued unpeaceful, perplexed, dark, and driven. I never spoke of this to Veronica. The carpenter, for whom I worked, sometimes planed cross-pieces for crucifixions. It started with my helping him to smooth the wood. Then, too, there were times when I found myself lost in contemplation of one of the cross-pieces as it leaned against the wall of the workshop. Later, I began to ask to go with him to deliver these now-fascinating objects to the executioners. finally, I took to watching and sketching every crucifixion that took place in Rome. Also, I became a collector. I acquired used crucifixion nails and cross-pieces and the signs naming executed criminals. After a few years, the wood of crosses was all I would use for my statues.

I will try to tell why I kept all these things hidden. I believe I would have told Veronica, had it been simple guilt, a simple sense of having failed my Friend, that drove me to the crosses. But the feeling was worse than that. It was a feeling of wounded professional vanity. I had missed my chance. I had been consumed with the need to describe the face, the look of Jesus, and I had missed my only opportunity. That look could have been there indelibly, utterly, for me to capture only at the cross. You see, I had learned by then that there are only certain moments when enough of the spirit has gathered itself into a particular body for someone like me to have a chance at making a true portrait. I had realized that on the boat, watching the Romans gather on deck to catch the first sight of their own land. Looking at their faces, at the yearning in their bodies craning toward home, I realized that I had never really seen a Roman before. With Veronica, one had to catch her reaching out to help someone. It was a fleeting moment, difficult to capture. With Jesus of Nazareth, it would have been the cross, but I had not been there to see.

It was one wet end of winter when I noticed that Veronica no longer left her bed. We did not speak of it, but I worried that she might feel trapped by her illness, so I began to carve her a substitute world from my bits of wooden crosses. I remember best the birds because, after I carved them, I hung them from the ceiling as if in flight. I made pigeons, and bluebirds, and nightingales, and sparrows, and warblers, and a great Roman eagle with blood-tipped wings. Veronica loved this last because she said the red was an improvement which proved that her world was not only as various as the one outside, but different and therefore uniquely superior. There were animals too: squirrels and rabbits tucked into her bedclothes and a fawn standing at the foot of the bed, as if listening for someone.

My friend brought me the wood now, as well as the news of crucifixions. I no longer left Veronica. We had so much to talk about in those days. She had so many thoughts about each of my carvings, so many ideas for new animals for her world, so many memories of moments in Jericho and Jerusalem, moments that I could bring alive simply by carving a dragonfly and hanging it just there in the corner at an angle just so. She also told me all the things about Jesus that I had failed to hear when she had first told me long before, when He was still among us. She told me too about her dreams: that she and I returned to Jerusalem and met two people named Susanna and Zaccheus. In her dreams, we liked them and comforted them, and became friends. Sometimes, at the end, we would take them home with us to Rome, so they could be safe. It pleased me to think that Zaccheus might have survived, might have a life of his own still somewhere. Zaccheus had been a poor, rabbitty, muffled-up sort of a person and I liked to imagine meeting him by chance and surprising him with some small kindness.

It was Veronica who begged me to leave her to go see the executions of Peter and Paul. She said that only I could watch closely enough to describe to her every detail so that she could understand what had really happened and think about what it meant. "Some things are important," she said. "We don't understand why all at once, but we have to keep watching even if it's not clear yet what it is we must see."

So it was that I went, and in my sketches that day of Peter crucified, I was finally given that portrait that I had begun in the tree in Jericho. I knew with the first few lines that I had seen Him at last. Still I could not stop watching. I remained and watched and saw the body's last breath.

When I returned to our room, my first thought was that bandits must have entered, stolen everything, and murdered Veronica. She lay cold and already stiffening in a bed filled with blood. All the singing birds, the small animals, the flying insects, all the world I had built for her, all had been taken.

For some moments, minutes perhaps, all I could think of was punishing the monsters who had ravaged my world. Nero was Caesar now of a Rome where men like Peter were crucified and where dear helpless persons like Veronica were robbed and murdered in bed. Even worse, it was I who, in my selfishness, had brought my love to this Roman hell to be slaughtered.

Some mindless habit within me moved me to pray. I stood at the window and looked up at the sky. This was how I had begun to pray, long before I knew it was praying, when I was working on the first misbegotten statue of Jesus. In those first days I would try to stand in the way that Jesus had stood looking up at me. At the beginning my praying was simply trying to imagine where the ears should be placed on the statue, and how the shoulders should lie.

This time, standing so, I saw an eagle circling overhead, an eagle with red-tipped wings. In the street below, I heard a maiden drop both her buckets. Looking down, I saw she had collided with frightened fawn. A sparrow alit on the windowsill and looked at me as if waiting for some sign of recognition.

Then I understood that the blood had been caused by the bleeding of the White Sickness. You see, I had gotten into the habit of forgetting about Veronica's disease after Jesus cured her. So, there had been no murder, no looting. My creatures had simply not been able to let her die alone. The rabbits and the squirrels must have come closer to rub against her and keep her warm. The birds would have perched on the pillow to hear her last words and sing her to sleep. The dragonfly, I know, was before her eyes as they dimmed, tilting for her at just the right angle as the fawn walked forward to say farewell. I thought, too, that she had probably died on purpose while I was away, so as to spare me experiencing a death I could not yet understand, and to take a first-row gallery seat at Peter and Paul's execution, because it was something important for reasons one did not know yet, but one must still be there to see.

After that, I simply followed the eagle. He took me a long way. I had to buy a boat. This rock where we have paused is somewhere in Gaul, I believe. The eagle is still with me. I love to watch him soaring along, lifting on the winds between my Rock and the other rock that bounds this valley. When I first arrived, I finished the carving of Peter crucified. Since then I have carved only my cave in the rock.

My poet believes me to be a saint. I try to explain that I am merely a person who carves the things that he sees. Just now, it is a hole in this rock that I am seeing, so, here I am, carving that thing.

The poet was just examining that old statue of Peter. He turned it upside down and said it was Jesus, and was carved out of the true cross, as well. I said nothing. I no longer try to tell people which true images to see, and I have seen enough crucifixions to know that all of them take place on the true cross.

The poet says too that the carving of Veronica, the one I keep always with me, is a statue of the Virgin. "It is Veronica," I told him.

"Yes," he said, "I knew it at once, the True Image of the Virgin Mary. You must have looked on her with your own ancient eyes."

"Veronica," I told him; I still love to say the name. Someday she too may awaken, like the eagle, and then she will tell us all her own true name. At least now I have written the story. Veronica always said that ordinary people would have to hear the story first; after that, they might see.

POSTSCRIPT

In Rocamadour, a small village in the south of France, there are cells carved out of the sheer rock. In a chapel at the top of the rock they keep an ancient, detailed carving of the Virgin. The villagers say it is a true image, and that Amadour must have known Mary face to face. Some even say that he was her slave.

ROMAN MARTYRS, DESERT FATHERS, FATHERS OF THE CHURCH

VALENTINE

VALENTINE'S HOUSE

His house was perfect, whether you liked food,
or sleep, or work, or story-telling, or singing, or just sitting or
thinking best, or a pleasant mixture of them all.

—J.R.R. TOLKIEN, *The Hobbit*

There the conviction was suddenly borne in upon me
that Christianity is preeminently the religion of slaves, that slaves
cannot help belonging to it, and I among others.

—SIMONE WEIL, *Waiting for God*

VALENTINE

Most of the fourth, fifth, and sixth grades I spent in Ancient Rome, mostly in the Roman baths. I had painted the ranch's claw-foot bathtub red and the bathroom was small enough to steam up, making it seem foggy and vast. Towels became togas. I lay on my stomach on the bath mat reading *Last Days of Pompeii* and imagining I was on the heated floor of the natatorium, hobnobbing with all the people in that book and in others: *Ben Hur, The Robe, I Claudius.* One of the fine things that has made it almost worthwhile becoming a grown-up was actually bathing in such a place. A real place, not imaginary. Or perhaps a place that was both real and imaginary. It was in a small town in Japan where not a soul spoke English, much less Latin...but you really could swim and there were cold baths and steamy ones and rooms to stretch out in and read or converse or watch X-rated cartoons on television. (I do think the Romans would have endorsed this last had they known of it.)

Valentine I met even before I fell in love with his city. When I was four and living in New York City, my father on great occasions took me to Sunday school at Riverside Church. He was a relatively penniless student at the time, and this was one of many free pleasures we discovered, along with Grant's Tomb, Central Park, hanging around the delicatessen, and watching the ice skaters in Rockefeller Plaza. One day in Sunday school someone told us the story of Saint Valentine. I was very, very little, so I doubt that I had the story straight even at the moment of hearing it and loving it. Certainly, I didn't get it straight enough to retell it, not to my mommy and daddy, not even to myself.

Ever since, I've been trying to reconstruct the story I heard that day. I sat in the British Museum Library for days surrounded by piles of books about Valentine. I learned lovely things, like that in the early church, members drew names each year on Valentine's Day. You became the "Valentine" for the person whose name you drew for the entire year, showering Christian charity upon them by whatever means you could devise, preferably in secret. A charming custom, truly, but not the special true unrememberable story I had heard when I was four.

On my youngest son's fourth birthday, we took him to Disneyland. It was a long-awaited treat and every step of the preparation and journey heightened the pitch of our delighted excitement. However, when we arrived at Los Angeles International Airport there was something wrong with the noise the crowds were making, as if a hive of bees had gone mad. There had been a tornado. Everywhere streets were flooding, and rain was still pouring down. Southern Californians were decompensating as absolutely as only those who live too long in Paradise can.

It was very dark, black in fact, and we had to wait a long time for the bus to Disneyland. The driver had to take the long way around; even so we went through many partially flooded streets. Even for me it was a little scary, and my small son's face had gone white.

That was when I began telling him the story of Valentine. It was a long story and somewhere in the middle I noticed that the other children around us had gotten quiet and were leaning forward as if afraid they might miss something, which I'm afraid they did as I'm not sure I had the story right that first time nor if I've got it right even yet.

VALENTINE'S HOUSE

The first thing Valentine remembered understanding was that the house belonged to him and he to the house. Also, that the house was perfect. Set in a series of immense gardens and vineyards and fields that stretched all the way to the Tiber, the house was like white filigree, patterned and fringed with courtyards and long colonnades. A largish stream wound through the estate, and there were springs, one in particular that overlooked the river and which had not yet been elevated to a marble fountain, but appeared alone out of the mysterious insides of a hill and ran down a long trail of dark moss. There was a canal, too, and a rowboat in which you could glide quietly alongside the Tiber, and there were goats and geese and a wine press and a wrestling ground and an old Etruscan tomb.

To the orphaned Valentine, the vast house, manned as it was by a dozen useful and omniscient slaves, was more than a family; it was a world. It offered endless preoccupations: which herbs and trees to plant and where? Which formula to use for making cheese? Which designs to choose for the new frescoes decorating the steam room and the bath? Then there were the parties, long dinners under stars with carefully chosen musicians and acrobats and clowns and storytellers weaving through the silences when guests, reclining in clusters of six or nine, looked up into the sky and talked lazily or tried to remember the words of some old song or the name of a star.

Valentine dreamed often about his house and had made a pact with himself that whatever appeared in any of these dreams, he would make real as quickly and precisely as possible. In this way, his dreams had brought an olive tree (which lived but rarely bore fruit), willow trees by the canal, and turtledoves and lambs and a caged lion and a new sort of goat that was black as night with evil eyes.

So, when Valentine dreamed that he saw the large light-domed central atrium bare except for plain wooden benches pushed against the wall, and lit eerily and forcefully by a mass of candles around the fountained center, Valentine went to the atrium and did just that to it. He was standing near the candles marveling at how perfect it all looked when the old slave Aurelia fell on his neck sobbing with joy.

The next thing he knew the slaves were all hugging him and kissing him and hustling him down to a smaller secret room below the baths near the furnaces, a stark room with a mass of candles in the center and benches round the walls. Aurelia admitted having baptized him a Christian when he was just a baby, and Valentine slowly understood that they had mistaken his actions as some public statement announcing himself as one of them, a Christian. He felt it would be rude to disillusion them; rude, crassly insensitive, and unworthy of his house. Valentine explained it all to himself, silently deciding that the dream had probably come from those half-remembered infant days when the slave women held and rocked him during their strange services here in the basement room.

In being merely polite, however, Valentine embarked on a course which led him to more and more wonders, wonders which, like the dreams, resonated perfectly with the house. There was the Christian music for one thing, lone voices with no instruments, a lovely searching sound that the house seemed to have been waiting for. There was the Christian brotherhood, too, the continually surprising delight of having the slaves treat him as an equal. They now talked to him every day in that oddly familiar way that had once been restricted to the seven upside-down days of Saturnalia.

Saturnalia, December 17 through 24, had long been Valentine's favorite time of year. He threw long house parties at which everything happened backwards. The women came dressed as men, and the men put on women's clothes and adopted feminine manners and gestures. The guests arrived at dawn instead of dusk, and immediately went to sleep in the daytime and in the slave quarters. Valentine and his guests arose at sunset by torchlight and attempted to carry out the slaves' jobs.

Christianity had taken the house to a place where Saturnalia reigned in endless holiday. Here in his house the slaves never ceased doing all those things Valentine had been taught that they were incapable of doing. They creatively complained, they told jokes, they told him what they really thought, they gave him things and he gave them things back. It was wonderful.

What suited the house best of all were the Christian sacraments. These, Valentine learned, were recipes for the most perfect parties ever. The house would shine for a mass; it grew mellow and comforting when the ill and dying were brought to be anointed with oils in the large incense-steeped atrium; it beamed on christenings; but it was most glorious during weddings, which Valentine came to believe were humankind's most fascinating art form. Valentine never tired of the couple's small preferences, so shyly requested, yet so desperately championed: the guests who simply had to be there, the robes they must wear, the aching necessity for tiny yellow flowers, the one flutist from the north who was the only one who would do, the special words that must be said, the special birds which must be freed to fly at only that one special moment in the ceremony.

It was because of these passions that Valentine was made a Christian priest and also because he could never persuade his colleagues how vanishingly little he understood about their religion. In fact, Valentine didn't decide to become a priest as much as the house decided to become a church. Valentine kept trying to catch up, but his ability, or the house's ability, to make every sacrament come out perfectly obscured the fact that he had no real idea how he made all these things happen.

Valentine's former friends never learned to think of him as a Christian, much less as a priest. It would simply slip their minds. Time and again, they found it impossible to think of Valentine as changed or converted in any fundamental way. If anything, he had become more entirely himself, finally successful in his perennial preoccupations about the running of his house.

For a long, long time his life continued smoothly on, dreamlike in its odd beauty and constant vague confusion. Then one day the Emperor Claudius banned all marriages. Rumor had it that the Emperor had decided that marriage blunted a young man's appetite for soldiering. Valentine though this preposterous. In his experience, brides and grooms had insatiable appetites for all forms of folly, even war. Even as the wedding bells tolled, husbands began to find the idea of the legions suddenly irresistibly romantic and leapt off to join them, leaving their brides to make centurions for the next generation. One might almost say that weddings and war made a perfect match. Valentine thought the ban the most deplorable military strategy. In addition, the timing could not have been worse. February brides were ancients Rome's equivalent to our June brides. The Emperor's ban came at the beginning of a February, booked solid at Valentine's house with heart-stopping, once-in-a-lifetime, glorious, thrill-a-minute weddings. Valentine could not face canceling them all. His house would have been devastated.

After the first few days, word got out that Valentine was defying the Emperor. (Valentine himself would never have phrased it so ungraciously.) So, through the first half of

February, Valentine was performing weddings, sometimes two or three at a time, at all hours of the day and night. Even before this, it had become fashionable to have a Christian wedding at Valentine's house; most couples then changed clothes and went over to the Temple of Juno to tie the knot officially. (In Rome, it was actually untying the knot, for the groom cemented his vows by unloosing the bride's girdle.) This was exactly what Valentine tried to explain to his friend, the Praetorian, who came to arrest him in the middle of a quadruple wedding on February 14, the day before Lupercalia.

"They're not real weddings," he explained, "just Christian ones. It's a chance for an interlude of theater before they do the official thing. Surely it's only the official bit that's banned, and I don't envy you trying to regulate even that part."

The Praetorian's jaw dropped. "Oh, no—that had completely slipped my mind, Valentine, your being a Christian. You're sunk for sure now. Just this morning the Emperor issued a ban on Christians too. He says they're a threat to the Empire."

Valentine was amazed. How incredible that the Emperor Claudius, Claudius the Goth as his troops named him, should consider Christians a threat. Claudius, who was unmoved by Visigoths, Vandals, and scores of other wandering barbarian tribes of various stripes...unmoved by siege towers, amputations and Greek fire...this same Claudius began to shiver and shake when confronted by brides and Christians. Either the Emperor was mad or stupid, or Valentine's hobbies were far more dangerous than he had realized. Valentine kept turning all this over in his mind, too absorbed to take much interest in the mechanics of his own arrest. From the first, Valentine had understood the beauty, the maddening, uncanny beauty in Christianity. That it might also contain something terribly powerful, something violent, elemental, and terrifying was a possibility he had not even considered.

Valentine was jailed in a solitary tower near his house, in the Fields of Mars. He was to be held there during the seven days of the Feast of Lupercalia. Claudius had felt it might be impolitic to execute the only priest still performing weddings in Rome precisely in the midst of Rome's annual fertility festival. Valentine himself had never learned to like Lupercalia. He could never get past his distaste for the sacrificial killing of the dog. Valentine understood that the dog went to slaughter willingly; dogs were like that. but he felt nothing but shame as the Priests ran by, flogging the populace with strips of that poor willing dog's flesh. Others found it wildly romantic and fertility-inducing. Valentine preferred weddings.

And, in his prison, weddings became Valentine's hourly fare. The four couples whose weddings were interrupted by the arrest were the first of many to stand below his barred window and hear the words of the wedding service. Weddings were only one of the delights of prison life. Although Valentine was granted only seven days, 168 hours in all, of prison, it seemed to him that this time grew to become a second lifetime, a lifetime's equivalent of sensory delight. The first life, the life in his house, had been richer, longer, more joyous than any man could ask from the gods, but this second life, the life in prison, provided an eternity of varied pleasures.

The first thing that met Valentine's eyes after the Praetorian locked the door behind him was the image of his house framed in the barred windows. Valentine had been fantasizing for years about having his house painted, but never had he hoped for a portrait as complete as the one provided, as if by magic, from his prison window. He never grew tired of looking at it and came to realize that he had never really seen or appreciated or known the house as he came to know it now from this perspective.

The jailer's daughter, Hilaria, was a wonderful help to him in learning to see his house, because she was blind. Blind, she had seen the house for years by its music and laughter and voices and recognized Valentine immediately as belonging to it. Hilaria was also a wonderful cook and brought him bean soup, black bread, heavy red wine, roasted sheep hearts and many other exotic delicacies which the slaves had always thought too robust for Valentine's palate. So this second life, this prison life, became a mingling of the new beauties of his house with a never ending epiphany of new foods, all indulged simultaneously with a nonstop series of vastly improved weddings.

That first day, Valentine hesitated to carry through with a slipshod, makeshift finish to that quadruple ceremony that had been dreamed about and designed for such a different kind of time. It was windy. The couples had got muddy and they were shivering. The sky was grey and threatening. It was simply not Valentine's idea of a wedding.

"I'm sorry, brothers and sisters," he called out from his tower window, "but we can't have a wedding in this wind." The wind ceased. It became so still one could hear the ants crawling.

"Also, it's beginning to rain." A rainbow came out and framed the couples like the arch of a perfect church.

"And," said Valentine, "we can't have you marrying in these muddy garments." Their togas became as white as snow.

"Also," said Valentine, "there are a lot of little things about a wedding, tiny things, really, that I believe are important, essential, actually, even though on the surface they appear to be the merest nonsense. For example, there are the tiny yellow flowers…" A bouquet of just those flowers appeared in the hand of each bride.

"And don't forget," said Valentine, "the doves and the music." Suddenly there appeared a chorus of white doves around his barred windows singing the most delirious music, and Valentine glanced down and saw that things were looking remarkably like a wedding, so he went ahead and said the words most cheerfully, and the couples kissed, but then one bride, less happily bemused than the others, remembered and looked up and called, "But Father Valentine, the certificate!" Valentine turned to Hilaria and shrugged his shoulders, but

Hilaria thought she recalled a sheaf of old execution orders in a storeroom somewhere and brought them out.

Valentine felt again the miserable skimpiness of using second-hand parchment for a document so precious as a marriage certificate, so he and Hilaria cut the execution orders into special shapes: a heart, a cupid, a dove, a tree. On the clear side of each, Valentine penned the name of a couple and then signed, "From your Valentine." A dove flew in and carried each certificate to the proper couple, delivering the document carefully into the hands of the bride.

Valentine was ecstatic. He had never imagined a wedding so perfect. It was much more fun, too, having Hilaria and the doves to share everything with: the preparation, the unexpected happenings, the gloating over the rightness of it all. They were the perfect new friends for this perfect new life.

It was Hilaria who noticed how sad the house looked (sounded) with no one there to enjoy it. The slaves had all left when Valentine was arrested, and the house was dark and empty for the first time in its life. Then the doves came and told Valentine about the children who stood silently peering in at the gate. (Valentine had noticed on the first day in prison that he could talk to the doves. In retrospect, he thought that perhaps he had understood the language of the birds for quite some time before that, but had simply never dared let himself know that he understood.) The doves said that they often saw these ragged children there, looking through the iron gate at the house with lost eyes. So Valentine took the key from a chain round his neck and two doves carried it together to the small gloomy child standing nearest the padlock.

"After I'm executed," said Valentine, "the house belongs to the Emperor Claudius but, until then, it is mine to dispose of as I see fit." After that, he and Hilaria could see the house clearly again because of the shouts and arguments and other happy noisy sounds which began to be made there.

Valentine continued in this exquisite new delight for what

seemed like forever, and was in the blissful midst of performing a mass wedding when the Praetorian came at the end of the week to take him to die. Hilaria was surprised that Valentine stopped the ceremony obediently in midsentence. He turned to her with an urgency, an excitement that she had never sensed before.

"There is something I must ask you to let me try. Let me try to make you see again, to fix your eyes. I have known now for days that I could do it. I know it doesn't mean much to you, but please let me try. I've lived my life like a child adrift in a sea of small graces and miracles, never caring how it all was arranged or how its parts could be made to move. Now I want to know how it works, take it into my own hands and make my own miracle before I die."

Now, Hilaria did not, in fact, at all want to see the face of a world that had condemned a Valentine to be bludgeoned to death, and she told him this in so many words while the Praetorian was shouting for Valentine to get a move on and while the mass wedding was growing restless down below. But at last she gave in and threw her arms around Valentine, and cried and cried.

He touched both her eyelids and said softly, "You must not be too hard on them for killing me. None of us, not even I, understands to what pleasures they will be sending me. In my first life I was most happy. I believed myself possessed of great power, surrounded by the richest beauty in the world. I thought I could make myself and others most profoundly happy. But here, in prison, I've seen that in that other life I was like a beggar standing in the rain in rags and tatters. And today when I look down on this second life from death it will be the same again. What I never will allow to change, though," he said, "is how much I have loved it here, how very dearly I have loved every single minute here." He kissed her on the top of her head, and by the time she opened her eyes, he was gone.

She opened her eyes to the vision of Valentine's house

framed through the bars, and it was more beautiful than anything she had ever begun to imagine. There were doves, too, flying everywhere, each one carrying a cut-out Valentine signed in the Father's own hand to the happy brides whose wedding vows were now sealed and accomplished. Hilaria, who had dreaded seeing in a world where she could not see Valentine, found that she saw him now everywhere. In all his old favorite places, his presence was stronger than ever.

POSTSCRIPT

After Valentine's execution and for the duration of the ban on weddings, couples in love would come and stand beneath that tower, and if the wind stilled, and the rainbow came to stand over them, and the white togas and yellow flowers appeared, and the doves began to circle overhead, they would say the vows out loud together, and, if a dove came down with a heart-shaped valentine with their names on it, they knew their wedding was true and official.

Claudius, the Emperor, was thwarted on another front as well in those last days of his reign. Claudius had always coveted Valentine's house and longed to live in it all by himself, but by the time his Praetorians came to take possession, the house had been thoroughly infested and booby-trapped by the street urchins who had made it their home. The Praetorians kept putting new padlocks on the gates, but then some dove would come down out of nowhere and bring a new key for the new padlock to let in yet another new vile and disgusting street boy. Inside the gates, there were rope snares that landed one upside down, hanging by one foot from a tree. There were hidden pits that landed one neck-deep in vile mud. There were teams of small boys who would jump out at one from nowhere and tickle one until one screamed for mercy. Not to mention the eggs and rotten vegetables. It was humiliating.

In addition, the birds and the other animals of the estate—there was a lion that had got loose, among other dreadful beasts—all seemed always to take the side of the boys. Also, there was something odd about the weather, such that the Praetorians were always slogging through a combination of hail and rainstorm in mud and gale-force winds, while the boys always fought in the sunshine. The Praetorians agreed at last to lie to the Emperor, and say the place was haunted, which Claudius was by then more than prepared to believe. In this way, Valentine's house became the first park, which was, had it known such a thing existed, exactly what the house would have wanted to become in its old age from the very beginning.

You can still find that wild park marked off by signs with skulls and crossbones in suburban Rome near the unexcavated catacombs and buried basilica of Valentine. This is a saint who lived his life in the great city but who cherishes wildness, keeping guard over this small wilderness in the heart of his city just as he watches over those less tangible wildernesses at the heart of love and marriages and happy homes everywhere.

SAINT NICHOLAS OF MYRA

VOYAGES INTO THE
SNOW COUNTRY

Perhaps there is a secret life and a hidden
Society of Saints and Virgins of which the church is
ignorant....In this society the saints seem more
like us, perhaps even like our children.

—MICHAEL TAUSSIG,
Shamanism, Colonialism, and the Wild Man

SAINT NICHOLAS OF MYRA

WHEN I WAS WORKING WITH CHILD PROTECTION, that was when I began to blame Saint Nicholas for Christmas, for all the cloying, expensive, overoptimistic, self-deception that is Christmas in America.

Christmas is a terrible time in a child-protection agency because the whole world wants each and every hopeless broken family to get back together at Christmas, and have a nice, wonderful, happy, loving, successful holiday. The parents emerge momentarily from their chaos to demand this; the children yearn for it with all their broken little hearts; the powers that be insist upon it. This is how life should be, must be.

Only the workers realize all the things that can go wrong on one of these nice Christmas visits. Mother ruins dinner and her ensuing tantrum so enthralls the whole family that no one remembers to ask whether the children ever got anything to eat after all. The kids get caught on Christmas Eve shoplifting a box of cigars to give to their dad. Dad gets angry and takes all the presents out from under the tree and burns them.

I blamed Saint Nicholas for the parents' credulity and the children's credulity and the judges' credulity. All of them were hanging on to this belief that it is fun and happy and nice to give things to children. But in reality, what children want is a clean bed after they've thrown up in the middle of the night, and to raise fungus in vats on top of the furnace, and to paint their rooms maroon, and for you to drive them round their paper route because it's 5 A.M. and minus thirteen outside. All these parents had already been through this and had messed up in some horrible way each time one of these golden opportunities presented itself. But as Christmas approached they imagined it would be different. "Jingle Bells" would begin playing in the background; the house would be neat and clean and red and green; children would be smiling and grateful.

It was Saint Nicholas who had painted this false picture. I did not blame the Holy Family. They would have fit right in at our agency. "What do you mean you're not homeless? You had this baby in a barn, lady." "Is it safe to try to transfer the case to Nazareth? Or should we remove the kid right away?" "What do you mean, you're not his real father?" No way Mary and Joseph would have kept that baby if our agency had gotten its hands on the case, but at least the Holy Family inhabited our kind of story. It was Santa Claus who had created a Christmas into which our stark realities could not be made to fit.

The Church had already tried to help me with Santa Claus. It had determined coolly and objectively that Saint Nicholas did not exist. Phooey on that. People have tried giving me that sort of help all my life. They told me that same tale about the monsters and the bogeymen and the witches and vampires and ghouls and giants and ogres. Anyone who's seen the devastation one of these creatures has wrought and can still look you in the eye and tell you it doesn't exist is too big a fool to be of any assistance in your struggles. So I've had to come to my own terms with Saint Nicholas.

That's what this story is about. It's all the things I found out about Saint Nicholas that made me decide it is okay after all to let him into my house once a year. It's not his fault, I've come to believe, that nobody in our society understands him. That happens to some of the best of us.

As it turns out, Saint Nicholas's childhood wasn't so great. An orphan, he was only a teenager when, on the eve of Diocletian's persecution, the Christians asked him to be their bishop. Nobody else wanted a job that meant prison or torture or execution or all of the above. Nicholas was alone in the world and rich. Better he should go to prison than one of us, thought the self-satisfied parishioners who selected him. (This whole story was reenacted each Christmas for centuries throughout Europe. On Saint Nicholas Day, December 6, a boy bishop would be selected to reign until Epiphany, January 6, presiding over the church with that mixture of utter irreverence and utter seriousness that separates child bishops from the ordinary sort.) I can't believe that Nicholas any more than later boy bishops failed to see the mockery and exploitation behind his appointment, but he must also have believed that it was his destiny, and he said yes. As predicted, that meant he was hauled away to do time in prison and in the salt mines and in the torture chambers, but it also meant he was given time to do some good, and save a child or two.

You may already know the story of the three daughters who were about to be sold into prostitution by their penniless father. As I imagine the story, the father was one of those stubbornly proud men who would never have allowed Nicholas to ransom the daughters outright. Seeing his children's lives ruined was hard, but not as humiliating as asking for help. Nicholas's solution was breathtaking. He dropped three golden balls down their chimney, one for each daughter to use as dowry. As it happened, the sisters had done their wash that night (well-brought-up girls to the bitter end) and had hung their stockings out to dry near the fire. The part that was magic was the way each gold ball, after Nicholas dropped it, bounced slowly up from the grate and then spun off in just the right direction to land in the stocking of the appropriate sister. That's why we all to this day hang our stockings by the fire on Christmas Eve.

The story I want to tell now about Saint Nicholas is different from those famous ones. It's a story from near the end of Nicholas's life when he was already old and famous and beloved. It's about the time when Nicholas went as a delegate to the Council of Nicaea. That's the closest Nicholas ever got to history, real history as it exists in history books, and as you will see, he didn't like it or fit into it at all, so he retreated immediately back into folklore. What's more interesting to me than the historical question of whether Nicholas was really ever at Nicaea is the folkloric question of why we needed him to be there. The Council of Nicaea was like one of those last Christmases before everything changes and the old people die and the old house is sold and nothing is ever the same again. We don't accurately remember any of the disasters, just that last Christmas and the foolish things our favorite uncle did, and encoded in that memory is all that we have lost.

To see Nicholas in his brief excursion into history the year we must imagine is 325 A.D. The place is Nicaea, in Turkey, not too far from Byzantium, which has just been renamed Constantinople and is being massively rebuilt to honor its namesake, the Emperor Constantine, who has taken it upon himself to chair this council of bishops, although he is not a bishop and not even technically a Christian. He has not been baptized although he has seen a vision of the name of Jesus and had it emblazoned on his soldiers' shields and then had won a great battle. Of course, prior to that, he had seen a vision of the god Mithra and had that one quickly painted on everyone's shields; he won that battle, too. Constantine never got straight that the lesson to be drawn from these experiences was that he was a genius at winning battles. Instead, he believed that they gave him some sort of special expertise about religion. So, Constantine was chairing the Council, and the bishops did not complain. Constantine had just united the two empires, stopped the persecution of Christians, started drawing up plans for the Vatican in Rome and was building cathedrals and palaces galore in Constantinople. No, the bishops were not complaining.

Other delegates included Arius, an Alexandrian songwriter and theologian that Constantine thought had some interesting and forward-looking ideas; Athanasius, who thought Arius was a quack and a heretic; Eusebius, Constantine's biographer and some say apologist; and Nicholas, the bishop of a sleepy seaport in southern Turkey.

VOYAGES INTO THE SNOW COUNTRY

Nicholas was thoroughly sorry he'd ever agreed to come. He had believed himself to be free of illusions about the church, men, and power, but he must have kept a few old and treasured ones in reserve because now he could hear them crumbling. Part of it was speaking Latin all the time, which gave him a headache. Constantine didn't know Greek (although he could memorize it for speeches) or Hebrew, so Latin they spoke despite the fact that it was a tongue that contained none of the concepts they needed—Yahweh, Messiah, soul. As far as Nicholas could tell Constantine meant Mithra every time he said God. This was what made it so tricky trying to explain to Constantine the Trinity; he had not yet quite got a grip on monotheism. Not that the bishops had capitulated utterly to their illustrious guest. They still had some sense of themselves and had voted down celibacy, for instance, with a resounding no. Nicholas wondered what it was Constantine saw through those misty eyes of his. Certainly not the present. Did he see a world where each town would have a bishop, a centurion, and a magistrate? A church, a fortress, and a house of laws? Except the magistrate and the centurion wouldn't have to worry about the bishop because he would be celibate?

Athanasius strolled past and Nicholas called out to him. "About the pledge," said Nicholas. "You know I don't believe in it. It's telling our people from the outset that we doubt their sincerity. Some have risked their lives to be with us. To insist they recite a pledge demeans them and us as well." Athanasius had heard these arguments before, and Nicholas had heard his counterarguments. Christianity was moving into the lands of the barbarians, Huns, and Visigoths. If even Constantine couldn't grasp the Trinity, how could these barbarians begin the task of conversion without some simple statement of what Christianity meant? Nicholas took out some notes. "What do you think of this as an outline of the basics?" he asked.

"I believe," read Athanasius, "in loving the Lord my God with all my heart and all my soul and all my life and my neighbor as myself. I believe that if another man steals my cloak, I should give him my tunic as well. I believe that if another man strikes me, I should turn the other cheek. I believe that I should not lay up earthly treasures, but keep my stores in heaven where neither moth nor rust doth corrupt. I believe that God loves me and will provide for me as he does for the lilies of the field."

"Now, Nicholas," said Athanasius, "you know this is exactly the kind of thing we're trying to get away from. As long as we're identified as anti-war, anti-property, and anti-slave, we're doomed to be a minority religion, like the Jews. Constantine wants a religion that everyone in the empire can share. That's his vision, and it's a marvellous one, to think that someday every soldier, every peasant, every magistrate, every jailer, even, in the whole empire will be a Christian."

Nicholas muttered something about how the jailers he had known, even if they had been Christians, wouldn't be. He said that Mithraism did quite well as a religion for everyone to share—or emperor-worship for that matter, or witchcraft—but that Christianity was all together a different matter. Athanasius didn't quite understand and took the opportunity to change the subject.

"Have you spoken to Arius yet? He keeps telling me how much he wants to meet you and talk with you. His old teacher was killed under Diocletian. He respects what you've suffered. He'll listen to you before any of the rest of us."

"It's been my observation," said Nicholas, "that he doesn't listen to anyone, not even our master, Constantine. I would think it's that quality that has roused the Emperor's interest."

"I knew you'd understand. What Arius has to offer is style, razzmatazz, a little song and dance. Tell him that is fine. All we ask is to be able to go over his lyrics and check them for theology. We won't do violence to meter or rhyme with any of our alterations or deletions. Tell him that from us. You're both poets. You'll like each other. He'll listen to you."

This was about the hundredth time Nicholas had heard that line about both being poets, him and Arius. Why did they think of Nicholas as a poet anyway? He had loathed Arius on sight.

Athanasius had already hurried on. Nicholas motioned to Big Peter. If they wanted him to speak to Arius, Nicholas would try. Big Peter had been with Nicholas since the salt mines. The jailers had burned through Nicholas's thigh muscles so he wouldn't run away. They did that to prisoners they thought might be leaders. Nicholas could still walk a little with his staff, but Big Peter had gotten used to carrying Nicholas, like a doll, and that was faster. Big Peter was a gigantic Ethiopian who had been sent to the salt mines for piracy. Peter had a trick of looking blank, which is why the jailers decided he wasn't a leader. That was an error. A worse error was to suppose that Nicholas would use anything so simple as his legs to run for freedom.

Why had his thoughts got so knotted up today with the salt mines? Arius was the agenda now. Of course, Nicholas knew he'd never gotten over the salt mines. The injustice continued to rankle, injustice compounded of malice (theirs and his), misfortune (mostly his) and stupidity (mostly theirs, despite the haunting suspicion that there might have been some loophole, chapter before last, which would have got him off had he only found it). Nicholas had tried using Christianity on this sense of injustice and Stoicism and a little Platonism but as far as he could tell none of it had worked. It still tasted bitter as ever.

The business of talking to Arius was problematic from any perspective, but first came the practical difficulty of getting to him. Arius had deployed himself in the center of the town square where he chanted his verses and danced from dawn til sunset; he had deployed two hundred ladies from Alexandria around him, an expanding spiral of ladies who repeated every movement and every verse. This had been the sum total of Arius's participation in the Council, not that it had been entirely ineffective. Constantine had remarked more than once that the dancing reminded him of certain Mithraic celebrations he'd attended as a youth.

How to get to Arius through all those swaddling ladies? Big Peter just kept walking toward the center of the square saying "excuse me" whenever anyone bumped into him. Finally he got Nicholas propped on his staff approximately in front of Arius who was still singing and dancing back and forth. The song was one that had upset Athanasius. "God was, God was, God was," it went. "Before Christ was, Christ was, Christ was." It was a silly song and a silly argument, thought Nicholas. They were talking about the state of God's being millions of years before the creation of the earth. Of course Arius and Athanasius would have different notions about what was going on back then. The only madness was assuming that either one could possibly be correct.

"Come on, Arius, and talk to us," said Nicholas.

Arius kept up his chanting but aimed his next winding step more directly toward Nicholas. When he got right in front of Nicholas, he gave him a look of pure hate and said, "You're just trying to stop us dancing, old man, because you're a cripple. You can't stand to see us dance because you can't stand not being able to do it any more." That's when Nicholas hit him, right across the ear and down the cheek. Arius's face was all unbelief for a second and then it twisted into a seizure, and

Arius fell. Nicholas was never certain whether God sent the seizure to save Nicholas from getting hit by Arius or to save Arius from getting stomped into the ground by Big Peter.

By the time the physicians and centurions had wended their ways through all the frantic ladies to the scene of the crime, Nicholas was in Big Peter's arms again, except he wasn't really there. Nicholas could be that way for hours—just not there. Big Peter could tell those times by a certain lightness; he wondered where Nicholas went. It was as well he wasn't here now because they were headed for jail and Nicholas hated jail.

Where Nicholas had gone was to the Snow Country. He always went there when he was angry and now he realized he should have gone there yesterday or maybe the day before that, should have been immersing his anger in that icy absolute cool days ago, should have been clearing his thoughts in that clean whiteness, that snow as white and as pure as salt. Nicholas no longer remembered how he had first discovered the Snow Country. He was still young, just a child, and so burning with rage and injustice he was on the verge of abandoning himself to a screaming kicking bellowing tantrum...and instead he found himself riding through the snow on the back of a gigantic deer with tall antlers. For many years Nicholas thought it was a daydream, but once he was a grownup and a bishop, other people, often people he was angry about, started telling him about dreams where they had seen him, Bishop Nicholas, riding a deer through the snow. "How interesting," Nicholas would say whenever he heard such a tale while, inside, his compass needle was spinning wildly around, trying to determine which daydream was more real, the one where he rode around the snow country on reindeers or the one where he wore a red bishop's robe?

Nicholas was truly sorry he had slugged Arius. He hadn't done anything like that since long ago at school. It was just his terrible temper. And it was true he had never gotten over the salt mines. Arius was right about how much he hated being a cripple. Nicholas wondered if he should try again to confess about that curse he'd put on the jailers in the mines. He never figured out how he'd learned to do such a curse, and so efficiently and well. It wasn't anything he believed in or had been taught. Occasionally, one of these curses just came out of him, full-blown, and wended its way through time and history while Nicholas watched amazed, unsure he had really given the push to such an alarmingly beautiful engine of destruction.

It happened when Nicholas saw the jailers selling the prisoners' food when the prisoners were starving. They were all sick with hunger. The thought had come unbidden, immediate: "This food you steal never will profit you, not to eat and not to sell. It will only profit us from whom you steal. Each mouthful you take from us will make us stronger and more. Every mouthful you steal will make you weaker and less." That was how the curse went. Once stated it became just a question of watching it play itself out. The prisoners' food began tasting better, and even a few mouthfuls were completely satisfying. Food the jailers tried to keep in their cave turned immediately to maggots and rot. The box of gold pieces they had hidden away turned mysteriously into coals. (Nicholas had asked Big Peter about that box of coals at the time but Big Peter just looked blank.) Finally the jailers began to starve. They tried to eat, but the very taste of the food pained and nauseated them. They couldn't keep anything down. They retched and wasted and then they died. This was what Nicholas didn't quite know how to confess, and, besides, he was not sorry. Still, after all those years, he was not sorry one bit.

The jail they were taking Nicholas to now was the largest in all Byzantium. In choosing the site for the bishops' meeting, Constantine had wanted a nice forum, nice baths, a nice theater, but most of all, he had looked for a nice big roomy jail. This dark underground space contained as much diversity, heresy, intelligence, as much vision for the future as did that space up above where the conference was taking place.

At first the rumor went through the prison that someone had been arrested who thought he was Saint Nicholas. It took several days for the prisoners to learn to believe that this frail, boyish man, fighting a pitched battle inside himself against his fear of the darkness there and the jailers was the genuine original Saint Nicholas about whom so many stories were told and upon whom so many hopes were pinned.

Nicholas ended up holding a kind of court each day, and he was amazed at how many of his old friends and enemies had ended up here. There was the father of the three girls who'd been given the golden balls. The father had gone on to marry the Madame he'd promised to sell his daughters to. He'd felt he owed her something, and he was so lonely. It turned out they had a lot in common. He'd felt betrayed by his first wife. She'd felt betrayed by every man in her life starting with her father. They'd had a fine marriage and done fine business together. The daughters were broad-minded enough to let them visit the grandchildren from time to time. Then Constantine, with his plans for a holy city, had swept them up in one of his raids and dumped them in this prison.

Nicholas met again the judge from long ago, the judge who had the unfortunate habit of incarcerating the husbands of all his current mistresses. He'd done it again, and Constantine had not been amused. Nicholas had originally objected to the injustice; Constantine simply did not allow his minions to mix their pleasure with his business.

Over in a corner of the prison Nicholas came across the innkeeper, the one who did horrible things to little boys in a tub in his basement. The innkeeper was standing with his hands tied behind his back and a noose knotted around his neck.

"Oh, dear, my friend, I thought we'd stopped you," said Nicholas.

"Nothing stops me," said the innkeeper.

"But we told everyone your secret. Even the new sign I made for the inn showed you in the tub torturing those boys. And I told everyone that the meat stored in your basement was cut-up boys. Even though that was not strictly true, it was true enough, and more likely to be believed than the weird things you actually did."

"Nothing stops me," said the innkeeper. "Here they tighten the noose every time I even look at a little boy. It takes me hours of strangled swallowing to work some slack back into the rope again. That doesn't stop me either." Nicholas asked if the innkeeper would like to pray and the innkeeper thought not, but Nicholas said a few prayers by himself because he was grateful he had gotten those boys away as soon as he had.

Eusebius tells the story of how Constantine himself went down into the bowels of the prison to rescue old Nicholas and beg his pardon and kiss the wounds of his martyrdom. Arius was no longer in fashion for the moment and it was thought Nicholas might be. However, it didn't happen quite the way Eusebius tells it. It was a centurion who came, not Constantine himself, and Black Peter had to pin Nicholas's shoulders back to keep Nicholas from slugging the soldier. Nicholas had got it in his mind to stay in prison since that's where all his friends were, and since Nicholas had been too terrified to sleep at all since they'd got there, he wasn't being entirely rational. Only Big Peter felt the utter relief in Nicholas's broken body as they followed the centurion up toward the light and freedom. Nicholas was far far away into the Snow Country by the time Constantine's spectacle was staged and the emperor prostrated himself and kissed the twisted scars of the old bishop. Big Peter was glad it worked out that way. He was tired, and it was long past time for both of them to say their farewells to history, such as it was, and go home where they belonged.

Saint Nicholas of Myra

POSTSCRIPT

The Council of Nicaea rejected Arius and produced a Creed, still in use in both Eastern and Western churches, which includes none of Nicholas's suggestions.

Constantine achieved everything he dreamed of. A year after the Council he killed his wife and son: people said it was because he found them in bed together. Heaven knows they were lonely enough, Constantine's wife and Constantine's son. Heaven knows Constantine would have been quick enough to slander them both in any way that worked, had he believed his precious future, the only thing that he still loved, required their deaths. By the time he was baptized and died, he had killed off most of his blood relations. Some surviving sons then killed each other, but then a somewhat distant cousin was found who everyone had forgotten about killing, and this child did manage to do a creditable job of succeeding Constantine as emperor.

Arius spent the rest of his life in and out of favor. Fortunately he was momentarily in, when he died in a seizure in Constantinople surrounded by fanatically devoted followers.

Athanasius went to the desert where truth was truth and he did not have to argue with idiots.

Nicholas has asked to die several times over the centuries. He gets very tired paying such close attention to children and also because the injustice done to children makes him angry and the evil that surrounds them terrifies him so. He stays in the Snow Country nearly all the time these days. The reindeer help him and Big Peter and many others, too. In fact if there is someone whose goodness and anger and terror you particularly loved in life and especially miss, chances are that person has gone to join Nicholas smuggling good things to children through the wastelands of the Snow Country.

His body of course gave out many centuries ago. It was never of much use or importance, anyway, even though men kept trying to use it to trap Nicholas or hurt him or get close to him. Six centuries after that body was buried some pirate-merchants from Italy stole it and carried it home to Bari, and that's where it remains to this day. The bones live in a stone coffin, and for centuries people have been puzzled by the steady drip of clear cool water that comes out of the stone drop by drop. You and I are no longer puzzled, however. We know that it is the melted snow. Nicholas is still dreaming his dreams as he wanders through his own snow country, and it is the snowflakes from there that percolate through his bones and seep out of the stone of his sarcophagus, ending as melted snow in that sun-filled Italian church where men believed that they had trapped him at last. Except they are wrong. Nicholas is not there. All we have captured of him is a few bones and the snow that's melting from his escaping footsteps as he vanishes once again.

PAUL THE SIMPLE

THE HAUNTED INN

Life is like a night at a bad inn.

—SAINT THERESA

That Saint Theresa was one smart little cookie.

—TRUMAN CAPOTE

PAUL THE SIMPLE

THERE ARE TWO PAULS WHO LIVED and worked with the great Saint Anthony in the Egyptian desert in the fourth century after Christ.

The first Paul, Paul the Hermit, is said to have fled to the desert to escape the persecution of Decius in 250, the year before Anthony was born. Paul the Hermit lived in the desert for ninety years and died, so they say, at the age of 113. However, Anthony did not meet the old hermit until Anthony himself had been in the desert for fifty years, had collected a large group of followers, and had made the ascetic lifestyle so appealing that contemporary writers published strategies for parents to use to keep their adolescent sons from becoming lost to this new, bizarre cult.

Anthony's late discovery of the old saint may have had a salutary effect on the great man's vanity. By this time (the year 340) Anthony was an old man too and a brilliantly successful one. He had begun to think of himself as the inventor of hermitdom and all that pertained thereto: the struggles against tempting infernal apparitions, the fasting, the silence, the repetitive manual labor—mostly mat-weaving. It was a jolt for Anthony when at last he met the ancient Paul who had come to these same routines of life without benefit of Anthony's wisdom. Also, Anthony was constrained to notice that during all the years while, he, the famous Anthony, had been lecturing to acolytes and sightseers about the nobility of his life of solitude, Paul had been off in his own corner of the desert doing the real thing accompanied only by a raven, two lions and God. Paul the Hermit is remembered on January 15, and Saint Anthony on January 17.

The second Paul, Paul the Simple, posed a different kind of challenge to Anthony's vanity. This Paul made the eight days' walk into the desert of the Egyptian Thebaid to get away from his unfaithful wife and his dead-end job. Anthony said Paul was too old and too stupid to be a hermit. The Saint was too polite to mention that Paul was also of the wrong social class. Asceticism in those days, as now, was largely a pastime of the aristocracy, like fencing, polo, or philosophy. However, Paul would not go away. After he had stood for four days outside Anthony's cell without food or water, Anthony asked why he was so persistent. "Because I can't die anywhere else but here," answered Paul. This caught Anthony's attention as did Paul's capacity for work. Once Anthony overturned a pot of honey; Paul collected very drop of honey from the ground without picking up a single grain of sand. However, this untaught and uncouth disciple remained an embarrassment. Paul was illiterate and utterly innocent of scriptural knowledge. He repeatedly interrupted with dumb questions like "Did Jesus come before Isaiah, or after?" Anthony came finally to believe that it was good for his soul to try to answer these dumb questions. Paul the Simple is remembered on March 7.

Readers who are picky about such things will notice that the books say that Paul the Hermit died three years after Paul the Simple, not before him, the way this story tells it. However, those same books also mention that everyone was constantly getting the two Pauls mixed up. Also, 113 sounds a bit old as an age at death, and all these things happened over sixteen hundred years ago. It seems to me that after all these years, my imagination is as likely to get the sequence straight as any other device.

Just to make things more complicated for future storytellers there happened also to be two different Macariuses working in the desert with Anthony. However, thankfully, only one of them found his way into this story, Macarius the younger of Alexandria, whose day is celebrated on January 2, on the ninth day of Christmas.

Macarius was a wanderer with cells in many deserts, but he was a favorite of Anthony's and acted more or less as Anthony's greeter and bouncer when they traveled together. Macarius was also the perfect hermit, and all the best hermit stories are about him. They attribute to Macarius my most favorite saying of all from the desert fathers: that whenever a young hermit begins to ascend into heaven, bystanders would do well to grab him by the foot. Macarius believed that heaven was found not necessarily up above us but wherever we succeeded in freeing ourselves from the world. Real contemplatives, he said, are burning with such great love that, if it were possible, they would take every human being into their bosom without separating the good from the evil. Once when monks were arguing about how most Christianly to use a dead hermit's money, Macarius intervened and threw the coins into the grave. In Greek, the name Macarius means "happy." Macarius believed that only our attachment to the world gives it the power to make us unhappy. They say that he never stopped smiling.

THE HAUNTED INN

If you asked where the desert was, Paul would have pointed west just as, had you inquired about old age, he would have shown you the ancient peasant dozing at the corner of the bar. Which is not to say he did not know himself to be old and in the desert. Paul crafted these thoughts while he polished the bar, arranging them around himself like pawns about a king, listening to his wife on the other side of the door that never opened, as she shrieked on, propounding her own definitions of his predicament.

She was grinding through a kind of rhetorical catechism on the question of why Paul spent all his time at the bar. "Is it because this is how successful innkeepers manage? No. Is it because he is a lazy, stinking, revolting, decaying drunk? Yes. Is it because there are no guests at the inn so he has nothing else to do? Yes. And why is it there are no guests? Is it because, as he says, the inn is haunted? Or is this just another lame excuse for his vile and disgusting alcoholic torpor?"

Actually, Paul had never claimed the inn was haunted. It wasn't haunted, in fact. It was cursed, and Paul was the tenth generation of Sauls and Pauls to labor under that curse. It was hard work and he felt he was managing fairly well. What made this curse particularly challenging was the way its specifications altered with each generation so by the time one Paul found a reasonable way to cope, he died, and left his son to discover a brand-new plague.

All this started several hundred years before Paul's birth when Saul the Innkeeper turned away a man named Joseph and his wife. There was no room at the inn. What else could he do? What would any other innkeeper have done? So most of the family said…but Paul wondered if Saul had seen that the woman was in labor and knew for a split second that it was not the night for business as usual and then still shut the door. Pulses of evil like that have to be caught and contained at the first flash. If integrity gives way at that first crucial moment the malady can run right through the generations.

However, that first Saul never understood what had happened to him or why. It took a century or two even to begin to piece the catastrophe together. All Saul knew was that for the rest of his life there was nevermore a room at his inn. It was one of those dreams which come true as nightmare. Every time Saul turned around he looked into the eyes of a new customer. There was no room to breathe, no privacy for thinking. Guests came in and out so quickly and relentlessly there was never a proper chance to figure the bills or collect them. The customers devoured everything. Only scraps of garbage were left over for Saul and his family. The toilet was never free, much less the bath. Even when he left home for a vacation Saul was constantly surrounded by such great crowds and masses of people that he never found space at a table or a room at an inn. He was finally trampled to death in Jerusalem one Passover by a passing mob infuriated about some Galilean heretic.

When Saul the Second took over, the crowds disappeared. It was peaceful again. The family heaved a sigh of relief but then noticed that the inn was beginning to shrink. Patrons complained that the rooms were too small and then stopped coming all together. Saul had to bend double to get through the tiny doors. He no longer slept at night because of being scrunched up in his short, narrow, little bed. They were always hungry because no one could cook enough food in the doll-sized pots or serve enough food on the tiny plates that now furnished Saul's establishment which had reached such a size now that there was finally and utterly and always *no room at the inn.*

So it had gone generation after generation. One of the saddest Sauls was the Saul who woke up one morning to find that his inn had run away from home. He tracked it all across Palestine, scampering after its large unmistakeable shambling cornerprints, but it stayed always just out of sight, just a little bit ahead of him. It was his son who finally tracked it down here in the desert.

When Paul and Xanthippe married, Paul's father was still running the inn. Paul senior's ill fate manifested itself in the form of bugs. There were ants in the sugar and on the bread, bedbugs in mattresses and pillows, giant cockroaches patrolling bathtubs and sinks, worms writhing at the heart of every apple. Squads of crickets and mosquitoes took turns alarming sleepers who awoke to find spiders crawling up their necks. Patrons, of course, never paid their bills, but this situation was not well known in the neighborhood. Xanthippe and her peasant parents believed she was marrying up.

On the day Paul inherited the inn, the insects, that plague he had known all of his life, suddenly vanished. That day the inn felt so clean and so wonderfully quiet. Paul took great pleasure in simply being there, strolling from one room to the next. One moment Xanthippe saw him thus and the next moment he was gone. It was days before he returned, clawing his way out of the impenetrable oceanic infinitude that the inn had become for him. After two more terrifying voyages into a vastness from which he crawled as disoriented as a ship-wrecked sailor, exhausted and perishing from thirst and despair, Paul did not enter the place again.

He built a bar onto the side of the inn. He learned and polished and watched over that bar's every inch. The bar was where he ate and slept, the one place where he knew himself positively and always to be found. When customers asked to stay the night, he made excuses. This was not difficult. He could offer three hundred accumulated years of reasons for not staying at this particular inn.

Xanthippe did not understand. She never became lost in the inn's internal intricacies. Xanthippe knew her place. It was not her place to clean the floors or tend the inn or show guests to their rooms. It was her place as wife to remain steadfastly in her own quarters waiting for Paul to do his duty. Knowing her own place so well, and holding so fast to it, she was immune to lostness, and Paul was never quite able to explain to her the perils of his position.

So it was that they spent their lives together on opposite sides of the wall shouting insults to each other on occasion. For a time Paul had expected that she would go off with one of her lovers and begin anew. It would have been her right. Now, however, he thought they would simply go on like this forever with Xanthippe screaming at him and him trying not to pay attention.

He was at the tail end of that bleak thought when he heard the knock upon the door. Or was it a scratch? Knock-scratch, knock-scratch. Then nothing.

Paul opened the door to find two fully grown lions, leaning against each other, each with an arm about the other's neck as if they had already drunk a few too many. They were smiling bright pink lions, with black bow ties, who strolled in, nodded to the old man in the corner, and settled their paws comfortably onto the bar.

Paul was worried. They might ask for a room, and they did not look like the kind of customers to be put off easily. He found some deepish saucers and poured them each a beer which they affably lapped up, then wiped their mouths, one with the right and the other with the left paw. They were beautiful to watch doing everything in perfect synchrony, the one the mirror of the other. They looked at Paul then for a long time as if trying to place him. He wondered if he had met them before but was certain that he would not have forgotten those two at least so possibly it was someone else that he resembled. They kept looking at him for a very long time indeed and then back at each other. For a few minutes they seemed to be chatting to one another in some private language of muted growls. Then like two businessmen after a refreshing pause, they climbed down from the bar, padded back to where Paul stood behind the bar, and, workmanlike, they herded him out into the desert as one would a goat. Xanthippe still was asking and answering rhetorical questions at the top of her lungs, and Paul was not sure if she heard his screams.

Anthony's nose and forehead rested on the cool cell wall and his eyes were closed. The woman had been screaming venom into the desert now for hours. It seemed that Macarius had been trying to explain this horror for equally endless time. Women almost never came to the Desert of Hermits but when they did come they always left immediately as soon as Macarius explained that they were not allowed. Men weren't really allowed either, but women were not allowed the most, but this one, who was worse than Anthony's worst fantasies of women, was not following the rules.

"The lions are pink," Macarius was explaining. "I am sure they are the ones who lived with the old hermit Paul, the Paul who died last winter. This old man is called Paul, too, and he is skinny and wrinkled like the old hermit, a simple-looking old man, sweet in a way like the other one was. The lions treat him like a pet. They've installed him in their old hermit's cave. They feed him by hunting, and the same ravens who brought bread to Paul the Hermit have been pressed back into service to feed this new Paul. The lions take him for walks letting him ride piggyback on their shoulders and they water him at the spring. At night they take turns watching him. In the day they lick him and groom him, and they are trying to teach him to pray and weave mats from the leaves of that date palm at the door of the cave. The pet seems not to mind these ministrations. He was an innkeeper, it seems, on the main road, and there was some problem at the inn which I cannot completely understand, but this old man thinks it was because God lived there at his inn and he says that was too close and he likes it better in the desert because it's farther away from God. He says now that he's this far away he might even come to like God a little."

Anthony would have raised an eyebrow but both of his were pressed against the cave's wall and the shrill female voice had just launched into a detailed answer to its own catechismic question of why Paul never had dared to enter his marriage bed. Anthony wondered if there might be some way actually to enter this wall.

"The wife doesn't like it," Macarius went on.

"Make her go," gasped Anthony. "Make them both go."

"I think the woman will leave on her own," said Macarius. "She hates to watch the lions loving him. I don't know about the old man though. Sometimes he looks like he belongs here."

Unobtrusively, obliquely, Macarius kept track of his friends. Months, years might pass without a word but somehow just on that day when you happened to be thinking of him, wishing he were there, Macarius would appear.

Paul had not been dead long when Macarius arrived. The lions were still digging the grave beneath the tall date palm. They were weeping so heavily that their tears had turned the desert into a large mud puddle. Anthony was kneeling in the middle of this puddle weaving mats. Anthony always wove mats when he was sad. Macarius counted three hundred and seventy-two mats in the present pile which meant that Anthony likely felt as lost as the lions. Macarius was remembering when Paul first came to the desert. Back then the lions thought he was their pet and Anthony thought Paul was his misfortune, and that was rich and fascinating enough, thought Macarius, just the way we all were that first day, but Creation was truly infinite, encompassing that first and this last and all the changes in between. Thinking of all this, and feeling the warm vast pleasure of it, Macarius began to laugh. He laughed and laughed which is not what most people do at funerals but this time it stopped the lions from weeping which was a good thing because if they had kept on, all North Africa would have turned into a mud puddle. As it was, their tears were so many that they dripped down through hills and mountains of desert sand and filled the hidden caverns far below. This is why, even today, secret wells and oases can be found in the Sahara and its sister deserts.

The lions had arranged Paul's body on one of Anthony's mats, his hands folded round a large black key. Macarius wondered if it was the key to the inn and he wondered if Xanthippe would miss it. Would she even miss Paul? Was she still at the inn or had she gone out into the world to make a life of her own? Had she changed as much as the rest of them had? When Macarius set off after the burial to find out, he was surprised to hear the lions padding along behind.

At the inn, Macarius found Xanthippe's dead body laid out just as carefully as Paul's had been. Her hands were closed around the twin of the key he had seen in Paul's hands. However, all the doors to the inn were now open. Keys were no longer necessary. Maps of the inn, sketched by Xanthippe, were taped in each room and corridor. Each featured a red arrow indicating where you were now. Many interesting people were wandering about, but no one looked lost. In Xanthippe's hands the place had grown uncursed and wholesome and then had kept on growing until it became rather wonderful. The place was still a hostel but it had become more than that, a kind of hospital and library and museum. Some rooms were occupied by visiting relatives of the Desert Fathers, some by lepers. A fellow named Athanasius had checked in and was collecting materials for a life of Anthony. In one room, someone had collected memorabilia of the inn's history: the door that the first Saul had shut in the faces of Mary and Joseph, a painting of the inn when it was so crowded with people it seemed to be bursting, some tiny dishes and pots, a fossilized footprint of the inn from the time of its wandering, some giant cockroach exoskeletons, and Xanthippe's sketches for her first maps of the inn. There are relics, too, of the other five plagues of the inn which I haven't even had time to mention—the plagues of fires and food poisoning and noises and floods and weathers.

Xanthippe's wake was thronged by the grateful travelers she had befriended. Macarius found himself eating his first hot meal in forty years and the two lions, seated majestically at the door of the inn, where they remained forever after, were brought beer in deep saucers.

POSTSCRIPT

That vast peripatetic inn which once had no room now has rooms and branches and annexes all over the world. Some of them are easy to find, the ones with large stone lions guarding the doors to remind us of the lions who guarded Paul the Simple. You may have explored already some of these more easily identifiable branches of the inn: the New York Public Library, Trafalgar Square, the Chicago Art Institute. Ordinary people bustle in and out of these places as if the lions were made of stone, but now that you know the story and understand how starved these lions are for human contact, hopefully, you will have a caress or a kind word for them and remember on Christmas and their birthdays how much they love beer. Other rooms of the inn are harder to find. You must learn to know them by the way you feel, and try to keep people who don't know from breaking down the walls for firewood or to build parking lots.

I can always tell when I've found one of these rooms because time stands still there, treading water, and because I feel like staying there forever.

ROYAL
CHILDREN

DYMPHNA AND GEREBERNUS

THE LEGEND OF SAINT DYMPHNA

Alas we know not anything.
I only know that good must fall
At last far off, at last to all
And every winter turn to spring.

—ALFRED LORD TENNYSON

DYMPHNA AND GEREBERNUS

THE BELGIAN VILLAGE OF GHEEL is mentioned in almost all textbooks about community psychiatry. It's not really a village any more, but a middle-sized industrial town. I came there by train on an April day so cold, mud-slogged, and endlessly raining that I had to wonder at the utter madness and futility of ever fighting wars in this particular corner of Europe. The town is dominated by a state-run mental hospital, a hospital like no other not because of its looming walls but because of the way its inmates escape them. In Gheel, patients can be adopted by local families; they spend holidays or weekends with these families, acquiring a bed and chores and companions, and participating in the family's small worries and odd habits and private festivals. This still takes place, despite the fact that nobody else in the world does it, and the late twentieth-century belief that altruism is obsolete. The practice continues because it has been done this way since the seventh century, according to legend, or since the tenth or eleventh according to historians. Villagers who fail to take in a mental patient face the same disapproving glances from their neighbors that we would if we did take one in.

The following story explains why. One time long ago a girl came to Gheel in trouble and a stranger. Like most of us would, the villagers decided she was crazy and a liar. Like most of us would, they kept their distance and went on with their own sane lives, but this time it turned out very badly. It turned out so badly they have never forgotten the discovery that she wasn't wicked or inferior, but just someone who had been hurt and was suffering. She was simply someone who had needed their help.

The church of Saint Dymphna looms as large in its way as the mental hospital, its newer counterpart. Some patients still circle the church nine times, telling and retelling the story of Dymphna, shown in the stained-glass windows. It is supposed to be a healthy story. Try it and see. So many stories nowadays seem not to be.

THE LEGEND OF SAINT DYMPHNA

Once upon a time a beautiful Princess lived on an island where her mother and father were Queen and King. The name of this princess was Dymphna, and from her birth she had been an amazing child, in beauty, sweetness, and cleverness.

Dymphna's father, King Coninck, was a cruel man and a pagan. As Dymphna grew older, she understood that the Queen disagreed with the King about many things. For one thing, the Queen was a Christian, and Dymphna too began to learn Christianity from the hermit Gerebernus who lived in a hut in the forest.

One day the Queen became ill. On Christmas Eve, just before she died, she called Dymphna and Gerebernus to her and said, "My daughter, I am no longer able to keep you under my protection. You must make your own decisions now. Gerebernus, try to guide her, with God's help." After that, the Queen died.

On losing his Queen, King Coninck sank into a black chagrin, becoming more cruel and strange than ever. His counselors, trying to cheer him, suggested that he seek a new queen. And so he sent his soldiers throughout the land searching for someone worthy to be his Queen, someone as beautiful, as sweet, and as clever as his dead wife. Alas, no such person could be found. When his messengers returned, the pagan King's mood became even blacker. Then a demon spoke to him. "What you seek is near you," said the demon. King Coninck, glancing up, saw his daughter, Dymphna. "There is the living image of your dead wife," the demon said. "She alone is worthy to be queen of Ireland."

The next day he asked Dymphna to be his wife. When she refused he thought, "She says this because she is shy, still a young maiden. She will come around to my view soon enough. It is the only reasonable thing we can do, now that the Queen is dead."

Each day Coninck made his proposal anew, at times stroking her body and using sweet flattery, at other times explaining why his way was right, and at other times shouting, threatening, and waving his sword in a rage.

At last Dymphna could bear it no longer, and went to the hermit Gerebernus for advice. "I wish my mother were here," she said.

Gerebernus thought for a long time and, at last, he said, "There is no way out except to run. All I can offer to do is run with you." The hermit told Dymphna that to gain time, she should ask the King to give her forty days in which to make up her mind about the marriage.

When Coninck heard this, he was overjoyed. He showered Dymphna with presents, and gave her dozens of fine silk dresses. "I will often be away from the castle," she told him. The King imagined that she was preparing for the wedding feast. In reality, she was preparing to fly.

One day she went out on her white horse and did not return. She met Gerebernus and an old couple who had been friends of her mother. They ran their horses as far as the sea where Gerebernus had a boat ready.

"My Princess," he said, "I do not know how to navigate, so I cannot tell you where this boat will take us. Do you still want to go?" Dymphna nodded and got into the boat. It was very cold and the sea was full of storms.

Not until several days had passed did the servants in the castle dare to tell Coninck that his daughter had disappeared. First, he had his soldiers search for Dymphna throughout his own kingdom. When he found that Gerebernus too was missing, Coninck decided that it was Gerebernus who had caused all of his troubles. "This hermit turned my wife against me, and probably poisoned her in the bargain. Now he has turned my dear Dymphna against me, and has taken her away." Coninck gathered a large army and began to search for Dymphna through all Ireland and then across the seas.

Miraculously, Dymphna's boat reached shore at the busy port of Antwerp, in Belgium. People came to stare at the old hermit and at the beautiful princess who wore torn, sodden, silken rags. She bought food for her friends with the Irish coins she had with her. Because she was beautiful, merchants "sold" her the food, even though her Irish coins had no value in Antwerp.

"Let us keep going," said Gerebernus. "There are too many people here."

They walked for many days into the forest. After a long while, they came to a shrine dedicated to Saint Martin in a lonely place with only fifteen houses nearby. The village was called Gheel (or Geel, pronounced like a gale of wind). Gerebernus liked Saint Martin, so they stopped and built a hut near the shrine. They lived there in peace for about three months.

Meanwhile Coninck and his soldiers searched for Dymphna, moving out in ever-widening circles from Ireland. In Antwerp, the King heard of the beautiful girl and the hermit who had arrived in a boat. Coninck sent his men to comb the countryside for more news.

It was Coninck himself who sat down to dinner one night at the inn at Gheel. "Oh, I cannot take this kind of money from you," said the woman who had served him. "I take these from the girl who lives with the hermit in the forest, but only because she is mad. I do it out of charity. Mad as a hatter she is, but lovely. Why, she says her father wants her to be his wife. She imagines it all, of course. She tells me that we must keep all this a secret. Poor girl. She believes, in her madness, that her father is still searching for her."

Coninck drew his sword and ran toward the hut in the forest. His soldiers followed. The woman at the inn was left holding another one of those strange unlucky coins.

It was the end of May now, and warm and light in the evenings. Gerebernus saw the soldiers coming and went to the door, hoping to shield Dymphna from them.

"You are the enemy," said Coninck, seeing Gerebernus. "I will kill you and be free."

Dymphna came to stand at the side of her confessor. "Please, for the love you have for me, do not kill him."

"And what will you do for me if I spare your friend?" said the King, reaching out to fondle her breasts. "What little favor will you do for your father then?"

Gerebernus pushed the King away. "The time has come to speak plainly, my King. No pacts with the devil are allowed. What you have proposed violates all rules of man and God."

The King spoke again. "Will you have me, Dymphna? In exchange for his life?"

"Never," said the Princess. King Coninck nodded, and a dozen spears pierced Gerebernus at the same moment.

"Now, my daughter," said the King, "Will you be queen of Ireland now?"

"Never," said Dymphna.

As always, the passionate lust of the King was very near to becoming a passionate rage. "You will be queen of Ireland, or you will die," he said.

"My father," she answered, "I simply cannot."

He nodded as before, but this time no soldier moved. He lifted his chin, his eyes blazing. Still, nothing happened. At last, one soldier walked over to Dymphna. He raised his sword. Then he let it fall again. He could not kill her.

Coninck strode over to where she stood. With his own sword, he cut off the head of his daughter.

Dymphna was surprised to find that after all of that, she was still thinking. Coninck had done all he could to stop her thinking, but even this last had not succeeded. She was going upward, very fast, and Gerebernus was with her. She stretched out her arm to hug her mother. "Dear Mother," said Dymphna, "Soon we will be together, but now I must find a way to bring Father with us."

Dymphna pointed down to where her father, the King, was trampling and hacking at what he could see of Dymphna and of Gerebernus. His demon had now gained possession over his self. Coninck slavered and howled, trotted in circles, and kept spinning his sword above his head. His soldiers backed away from him in horror.

Dymphna, who was learning to fly with more control now, glided down to hover behind the woman at the inn. "What have I done?" The woman began to think. "I thought she was just a mad, silly girl, but she was fighting for her life. How can I make up for what I have done?" Just then King Coninck came wandering in. Coninck howled at the door, then fell to the floor and settled down to writhing like a snake, and hissing. The woman at the inn went to him. "Perhaps I can care for this poor creature. He is guilty of much, but so am I. I will try to give him the care that I did not give to his child. This one I will treat as one of my own family, not as someone to ridicule or to point the finger at, but as someone who truly belongs with us."

Dymphna saw clearly now the demon riding upon her father's back. It looked like a small dragon with horns. She was amazed that she had never seen it before. She took the sword from her father's hand. The demon knew that she had recognized him and ran to hide under the bed. Coninck collapsed into the arms of the innkeeper, Dymphna kept stalking the demon. She hunted him for nine days before she caught him and stabbed him to death with her father's sword.

POSTSCRIPT

All this happened almost thirteen hundred years ago. Still today, if you see a picture of Saint Dymphna, she will be holding her father's sword and standing on the head of a vicious-looking demon. Gerebernus became a saint, too, and now he has long conversations with his friend, Saint Martin, every day. In memory of Saint Dymphna, today the families of Gheel still take in those who are possessed or deranged and help them to get well. You may celebrate Dymphna and Gerebernus together on May 15. Dymphna still helps to heal such people, as she healed her father. It is said that madness can be cured if one stays for nine days in Dymphna's church. Today, fathers still make passionate, demonic proposals to their daughters, and the daughters must try to find a way to say no. This is about as easy as slaying dragons. Dymphna and Gerebernus still wonder if they could have found a simpler way to do it. I like to think of the rudderless but willing Gerebernus, struggling unsuccessfully to keep his head, as the patron saint of all psychotherapists.

WENCESLAS

GOOD KING WENCESLAS
WENT OUT

It takes as much energy to be evil as to be good
and few people have enough energy for either course.

—ROBERTSON DAVIES, *A Mixture of Frailties*

Everyone exists in the very nature of suffering,
so to abuse or mistreat each other is futile.

—THE DALAI LAMA

WENCESLAS

Good King Wenceslas looked out / On the Feast of Stephen,
When the snow lay round about, / Deep and crisp and even;
Brightly shone the moon that night, / Though the frost was cruel,
When a poor man came in sight, / Gathering winter fuel.

"Hither, Page, and stand by me, / If thou know'st it telling:
Yonder peasant, who is he? / Where and what his dwelling?"
"Sire he lives a good league hence, / Underneath the mountain,
Right against the forest fence, / By Saint Agnes' fountain."

"Bring me flesh and bring me wine, / Bring me pine logs hither;
Thou and I shall see him dine / When we bear them thither."
Page and Monarch, forth they went, / Forth they went together;
Through the rude wind's wild lament / And the bitter weather.

"Sire, the night is darker now, / And the wind grows stronger;
Fails my heart, I know not how; / I can go no longer."
"Mark my footsteps, my good Page, / Tread thou in them boldly:
Thou shalt find the winter's rage / Freeze thy blood less coldly."

In his master's steps he trod, / Where the snow lay dinted;
Heat was in the very sod / Which the saint had printed.
Therefore, Christian men, be sure, / Wealth or rank possessing;
Ye, who now will bless the poor, / Shall yourselves find blessing.

FOR CHRISTMASSES AND CHRISTMASSES and Christmasses, I wondered and worried about Wenceslas. Who was this Good King Wenceslas? And why must we have a relatively unintelligible Christmas carol about him? Whatever and whenever was the Feast of Stephen and how had that become entangled with the story? Why did Wenceslas look out? Who was that poor man gathering winter fuel?

Of course, I've always been a bit dim about Christmas carols in general. My favorite player in the Christmas story for years was that chubby, kindly, jolly old fellow, Round John Virgin, who is unaccountably absent from manger scenes whenever I have sought him. I always thought that he must be some obscure relation of Long John Silver's, and the sort of grownup that a child would choose as a friend—mysterious, yet utterly accessible to a child's language and logic. No wonder that Jesus, even after he grew up, called John the disciple that he loved.

However, the Wenceslas carol perplexed me even more deeply. Now, after long years of patient and scholarly imagining, I know the answers to these questions, and now you must listen very carefully indeed, because you are about to learn those answers, too.

Wenceslas was born in 907, the son of Ratislav, Bohemia's first Christian duke, and his pagan duchess, Drahomira. Wenceslas was educated by his Christian grandmother, Ludmila, and her chaplain, Paul, the missionary who converted this noble frontier family. Boleslav, four years younger than Wenceslas, was Drahomira's favorite son.

This story begins in the fall of 921, when Wenceslas is fourteen. His father, Ratislav, killed fighting Magyars, has been dead for about a year, and Drahomira reigns as regent until Wenceslas shall come of age.

GOOD KING WENCESLAS WENT OUT

Boleslav had been crouched there in the corner of the parapet for a long time. Wenceslas knew, because he had been watching. Bo had brought up a huge pile of pebbles, then his model catapult, and finally, every single one of his tin soldiers. Now Bo was catapulting the pebbles into his soldiers, systematically smashing and killing them, one by one.

Wenceslas didn't like to interrupt him in this mood. It was just that he wanted so much to play, too. He touched the toy catapult dangling from his own belt. Young dukes were very much discouraged from playing. There were, in fact, whole hosts of things that heirs to dukedoms were not allowed to do. These days he was not even allowed to go see his grandmother. That was the thing he had come to speak with Bo about, bad mood or no bad mood.

So, at last he took a deep breath and broke the silence between them. "I hope you come with me to Tetin Castle this year...for our feast of the Day of Cosmas and Damian. It's only a little more than a week away now. Come, please, and help me guess about our present. Last year it was the catapults, and the year before it was soldiers, and this time it will be just as good, but grandmother won't give me any hints at all. I know you could guess it, Bo, you always do."

His back still turned to Wenceslas, Bo plodded on with the piecemeal extermination of his army. "It's forbidden," was all he said.

Wenceslas, though, was too much engrossed in his own persuasiveness to take the hint. "I've always gotten you there and back before." Wen was right. Ludmila, their grandmother, had been off-limits to the boys these months since their father's death, but the ban had not really changed things. Drahomira was not the sort of mother to waste time hovering around her children. They could disappear for days and Drahomira would never miss them. If she did say something, there were a hundred Christian serfs in the castle, Ludmila's partisans, primed to say they had just seen the boys with the blacksmith or in the kitchens or up on the parapet.

Wenceslas went on, irretrievably into the swing of his petition. "I like our Feast of Damian and Cosmas better than any Feast in the year, because it's all our own. No one else does anything special at all on that day. It's not like Christmas or Easter when we have to share the fun. I like it best, also, because it's exactly the same every year. First, grandmother tells us the story of the brothers, how Cosmas and Damian always worked together, how they healed the sick and cared for the poor, and how they died together, too, rather than betray their sworn fealty to their Lord. After that, we go to Mass in her chapel, and then we eat and eat for hours. The jesters come tease us and throw food and the mimers play. Then, at last, it's time for the presents, for our own treasure, just for us. It will be different this time, I know, doing it all without Father, but even so, it's my favorite day in all the year of days."

What Wenceslas thought, but did not say, was that mostly he loved the day because he spent it with his brother as if they were true brothers like Cosmas and Damian, undivided by different allegiances and different faiths.

"Please do come," Wen said again.

Bo's soldiers were all dead now, but he still sat hunched in the same way, as if he, too, were a catapult, with his string wound so tightly that his very self bent under the strain of it. Finally, he turned to face his brother. "You traitor!" he said, and then had to catch his breath to go on. "You *are* a Christian, and a traitor. I will not stand silent while our court proclaims you, a traitor, Duke of Bohemia; much less will I allow all the Czechs and Wends to proclaim you King. You would destroy us. I will kill you first, Brother, and with my own hands."

There was something about the way Bo turned his back this time that almost made Wenceslas forget he was a Christian traitor. With Bo, he sometimes felt like a very angry pagan. Wenceslas tried to remind himself that these scenes delighted Bo as much as the harmony of plain song pleased Wen himself. As he became absorbed in imagining what sort of pleasure that must be for his brother, he began to feel less awful. It was a bit demoralizing to be hated by one's own mother and brother, and sometimes Wen pretended they weren't related to him at all. Other times, like now, he pretended that what they were saying really didn't mean what it sounded like...

It was in the midst of this line of thought that Wenceslas began to run downstairs to the kitchens. It was dusk now, so he didn't have to hesitate more than a pulse or two before darting into the bread oven, the third one from the bottom of the steps, the one with the secret passage. After a long crawl, Wen climbed out of the tunnel and over some blackberry branches to reach the horse that his friends always kept waiting for him at that station of the journey.

By the time he reached the gates of Tetin Castle it was after midnight, moonless, and the two guards who should have been at the gate were not. The courtyard and hall were empty, too. Wenceslas started now toward Ludmila's own room near the chapel.

That was where he found her, lying dead on the high familiar bed. "Strangled," said Father Paul, who knelt with the old servant Podiven, praying beside her bed. Drahomira's henchmen would come back. Paul and Podiven had sent all the other serfs to find friends or hiding places in the forest. Now that the candles were lit, Paul and Podiven would do the same.

Wenceslas found the present in Ludmila's chest at the foot of her bed. It was a chess set this year, an exquisite one. The white pieces looked up at Wen with his own solemn mouth and innocent eyes; the black pieces seemed gloomy, like Bo when he had grown tired of waiting for a fight. Wen had time, before Paul and Podiven hurried him off into hiding, to take the stern white queen from the set and place it carefully in Ludmila's stiffening fingers.

September 27, 921
The Day of Cosmas and Damian

It had been an odder than usual week in Drahomira's castle. Not that this was saying much. Drahomira kept her court always on the raw edge of hysteria, but this week Wenceslas had not been seen at all, and Boleslav alone dined next to the Queen. In addition to Wenceslas, all the most powerful courtiers had vanished. If one asked, and no one liked to ask, Drahomira would say that they were out hunting. She said it as if she meant you to know it for a lie. The dowager, Ludmila, had been buried quietly by her Christian serfs. There were rumors afloat that perhaps Ludmila had died of something more interesting than old age, but no one paid much notice.

For the first few days, Bo enjoyed all of it most wonderfully. He drank in with an impartial thirst the attention, the deference, and the conspiracy. He had been aching forever for all of these things.

There dawned a day though, finally, that found Bo stale and restless and wretched. Nothing excited or pleased him. The prospect of presiding at the table evoked not even an echo of a thrill. He didn't even feel like eating.

Bo paced about the courtyard. He climbed around on the roofs and parapets. He slaughtered a few tin soldiers. As a last resort, he had his stallion saddled, and after an hour's headlong gallop through the forest, he felt more like himself.

He pulled up at a spring near the base of the mountains. The peasants called it Saint Agnes's Fountain, but Bo couldn't remember who Saint Agnes was. It was wonderfully cool here and deserted except for a ragged barefoot youth struggling up the mountain above, carrying a bundle of firewood. Bo thought he might just lie down on the ground awhile and look up at the sky.

That was what he was doing when, he spotted something hanging from the young woodcutter's belt as he staggered back and forth along the winding path. It was a fair distance away and Bo was drowsy, but there was a moment there, an instant only, when Bo was certain that it was a toy catapult.

Most likely, it was only a dream. That was what Bo told himself when he woke up. There was no need to mention it to Drahomira's bloodhounds, the score of rapacious nobles who had been scouring the countryside for Wenceslas with orders to bring their prey home dead. They would only laugh and tousle Bo's head and say what a fine little soldier he was. It had been a dream.

It was much later, on the ride home, that Bo realized that today was the Day of Cosmas and Damian.

As it happened, Wenceslas, at that moment, was thinking of Cosmas and Damian also. He was thinking that he and his brother might be like those twins after all. He had watched his brother sleep for a long time today. That was far the best way to appreciate Boleslav. Wenceslas had watched him so long that he had almost been able to see the invisible cord that bound them together, his brother and himself, to a shared task which neither of them understood.

DECEMBER 23 TO
SAINT STEPHEN'S FEAST (DECEMBER 26), 921

At dawn on December 23, the pagan lords who were now in command of Tetin Castle took their serfs and vassals and fled the castle's vast halls. By sunset only a few abandoned rats were left in possession of the domain. This was because pagans in those days believed that on Christmas Eve the Christ Child came to haunt all the Christian corners of the forest. Pagans who had trespassed near hallowed ground on those most solemn days of Christmas told of being pounced upon by a strange creature, part dragon and part troll. Some said they had been pursued by a chariot full of demons. If a pagan happened to inhabit a castle possessed of a Christian chapel and graveyard, it was highly advisable to plan a long visit somewhere far away at this particular season of the year.

To the great relief of the rats, Wenceslas, old Podiven, and Father Paul crept into the dark deserted fortress a few hours after its authorized inhabitants had fled.

There was a lot to do. What Wen did first was find the life-sized figures for the creche. That was the way Ludmila had always begun Christmas. The long hall looked so empty and even a bit spooky in the candlelight, so Wen decided to set the figures right there, rather than outside in the courtyard. Mary, Joseph, and the babe he put at the head of the table, then the kings, and the shepherds, and some knights and townsmen that the carvers had invented to people the stable, including one woodcutter. Wen felt particularly pleased to see the woodcutter again, now that he, too, worked at that trade.

It was before this splendid company that Father Paul made his report. He was arranging to have a council of nobles exile Drahomira and declare Wenceslas duke even though he was still underage. All the Christian nobles had agreed, and many of the pagans were interested too, as even they feared Drahomira.

The next day, and the next, there was more talk and also play and feasting. Wen beat Father Paul at chess, even though Wen had the whites and was playing without a queen. They bobbed for apples and then used the water to set afloat candles in sailing ships made of walnut shells. Each one watched to see his own little craft sail out his New Year's fortune. Wen's tiny boat sailed gracefully for a long time, then a candle's spark set it aflame and it burned and burned.

Father Paul left on the morning of the twenty-sixth, Saint Stephen's Day, after reading them the story of that first martyr. Stephen had been stoned on this day while a man named Saul held the coats of his accusers. Wenceslas had always wondered about Stephen. Had he felt ready to die? Was he surprised at the judgment? What most did he regret as he watched the stones come at him? Did he understand that his persecutor Saul would live to give more to his cause than Stephen himself ever could have?

Wen and Podiven should have gone in the morning, too, but somehow Wen didn't feel like leaving. It was such a relief to wear his own clothes again and act as the master of his own castle. They ate a bit more and talked a bit more, and looked longer at the beautiful carved personages who had come to share their feast. In this lazy, happy, carefree mood they lay down on the table before that fine company and fell suddenly into an unaccountably deep and dreamless sleep.

Wen was wakened by the baying of hunting hounds. They seemed to be all around him. It was dark. Podiven was still asleep, but the window had been opened. And there was someone else in the room.

"Silence," came a whisper from near the open window. "We have just enough time to escape, if you hurry." Wen shook old Podiven awake, and the intruder spoke again. "You must take off your fine robes and your shoes now so we can all pass as poor woodcutters." Rough hands took the robes and boots and the remnants of their feast, and moments later Wen saw their rescuer against the moonlit sky as he leapt down from the window and packed the bundle into a small sled filled with firewood. He motioned them to come out after him. Wen saw Podiven hesitate, looking suspiciously at the stranger, and with even more foreboding at the deep snow outside. In those first weeks of their exile the old page's disguise as a peasant farmer had allowed him boots at least. Wen saw that he should go first and let Podiven follow. Wen was used to bare feet this winter, even in the snow. He glanced backward just once at the long tables still peopled by carved revelers. Yes, one statue was missing, and it was the woodcutter.

All the way to the forest's edge, Podiven kept trying to catch Wen's attention. Something strange and wonderful was happening as they walked. Podiven cleared his throat, he pulled at his master's tunic, he whistled his special whistle. For some reason Wenceslas had become entirely engrossed in conversation with this unknown woodcutter. Perhaps, it was someone he had met in hiding, someone who lived near Saint Agnes's Fountain. By the time they reached the forest's edge and the woodcutter disappeared, Wen was too preoccupied to listen even as Podiven told how the snow had melted before him, how his feet were still warm, warmer than in summer sand.

Now, it happened that Boleslav was riding with the party of pagan nobles who reentered Tetin Castle that night. Boleslav had been appointed their guide and protector against Christian dragons and demons, and was relishing every flourish and nuance of his role. When the hue and cry went up about woodcutters sighted on the grounds, Bo explained that it was a Christian custom to give such privileges to the poor on Saint Stephen's day. On this one day, they were allowed to cut wood on the Lord's own lands. Boleslav, proud of his superior knowledge, could not have seen, even in the bright moonlight, that one of the woodcutters had a toy catapult dangling from his belt. Or could he?

SEPTEMBER 27, 929 (ALMOST EIGHT YEARS LATER) THE DAY OF COSMAS AND DAMIAN

Boleslav had been talking for hours. It was after midnight and he was still at it. The chamberlain decided it was time to assemble a new sleeping costume for his lord. The master did not like being forced to acknowledge that he was conversing and arguing with a mere chamberlain; much less could he tolerate being left alone in the middle of his obsessive monologue.

The chamberlain could recall times when he had dressed and undressed the master fifty times in a single day just as an excuse to keep him company.

"He is odd," said Boleslav. "No one can deny that. He holds feasts for beggars. I would disregard that charge as a calumny invented by his enemies, but I myself have seen him conduct one of the things. He goes about the town collecting beggars, fugitives, the filthy, and the homeless. The night I watched, he brought some of them up out of his own dungeons. At a pinch, he buys slaves from the East and feasts them, setting them free at the end of the evening. They are a motley lot, these parties. Of course, Wenceslas looks no better himself, barefoot and hairshirted. They say that one Saint Stephen's Day the King's guards caught him cutting wood in the forest and arrested him. His own guards mistook him for a poor woodcutter. He was babbling something about coming to that place each year on that day to meet a woodcutter from Bethlehem who advises him. I have heard that he makes with his own hands every item he serves to those creatures who come to his feasts. Our King himself, plants the wheat. He scythes and winnows this wheat, then mills it, and then bakes it into bread right there in his castle. Then for good measure he digs and molds and bakes the clay for the dishes used by these beggars, criminals, and slaves. This is odd, I tell you, and probably dangerous.

"In foreign affairs his eccentricity is surely dangerous. When King Henry of Germany invited all his vassals to a council, my brother failed to appear at all on the first day. When he finally wandered in on the second day, Henry asked what he wanted. And, do you know? Can you imagine what that fool of a brother of mine answered? 'A bone of Saint Vitus,' he said. And, Henry, flabbergasted, as would be any normal king...Henry gave it to him, and that is the beginning of how I am come now to kill him. You see, none of us realized at the time how clever it was, that request. It was fiendishly clever of him....The crowning injustice being that he still has no idea how clever it was. What he did, once he had possession of this awful bone, was to insist that each of his vassals swear fealty to him while touching the dreadful object. That would have been bad enough, but then, during the first ceremony, my most loyal Duke, the Master of Tetin Castle, fell down in an apoplectic fit at the very moment he touched the thing. That marked the end of my attempts at a political solution. No lord who had sworn fealty to Wenceslas on that sacred bone would even consider taking seriously my claims to the throne. They fear they would fall dead of the plague or something. Now that he has a son, assassination is our only option.

"It is the King, himself, who forces this measure upon us. Look what he's done to the army! The last hope of a war we had was when the Zlicaneys invaded. We were ready. We were in the right and could have driven them back home and beyond and taken their lands and castles and women and slaves. So what does my brother invent to spoil it all? A game of David and Goliath with their leader, the Duke! 'Let us settle this by single combat,' he says, and I knew right then that we were finished. I would have killed him then and there before the Duke did, except that a thousand eyes from each army were on him. The Duke said that Wen used magic to defeat him, and I saw it too that day. It must have been that magic cross he wears that pushed the pagan's sword away every time. Now each of our neighbors knows that if he invades, he faces a hand-to-hand fight against Wenceslas and his magic. So, war becomes a lost art in my own land. It's not fair. He takes everything away from me.

"He was happy tonight. Did you hear his toast? Very solemnly and formally he raised his goblet and said, 'May you ever prosper, Brother, and have abundance of all the good things of this world and the next.' Perhaps he believes he means that. Perhaps he could only know the hatefulness of watching another's glory if he had to be a minor noble in the suburbs, while watching *me* play king in the capitol. Now he suspects nothing. This day is precious to him. I arranged everything as he's always dreamed it. We read the story of the brothers. We feasted amid jesters and mimes. We played chess. The fool! He plays without a queen. Tomorrow we go to Mass together. He is very happy."

SEPTEMBER 28, 929
THE DAY AFTER COSMAS AND DAMIAN

It went like clockwork. Like slow-motion clockwork. Almost. As the brothers dismounted before the church, Bo unsheathed his dagger. Only the utter calm anticipation in Wen's eyes unnerved him. There was no fear, not even surprise, only a kind of knowing sorrow. "To do this would be evil," Wen said. "May God forgive you as I forgive you." It did not matter. None of it mattered, because two of Boleslav's mercenaries stabbed the King in the back at that moment. Old Podiven killed one of them, but that didn't matter either. Podiven was one and they were many and he would hang for his interference.

Once the deed was done, Bo's men fell to the tasks at hand. For one thing, they had to check and make sure the King was really dead. With magic afoot, who can be certain? There was no cross beneath his shirt today. That was luck. Instead he wore some kind of wooden toy around his neck, something like a small catapult. In all their hurry and new-found self-importance, it was a long time before they noticed that there was something wrong with their master.

Boleslav had crawled to the church door. He was kneeling there, scratching methodically at the lock. No one liked to interrupt him in that mood, but his fingers were already bloody. They could understand nothing in the stream of words he was babbling.

Boleslav was thinking how foolish he had been to lock the church. It had seemed such a masterstroke at the time. Lock the church and the King will be prevented from seeking sanc-tuary. But Bo had forgotten. He always did have so much trouble remembering how Wen really was. He hadn't even remembered about Wen's wife and baby. Of course, he knew about them, had attended the wedding and the christening, had calculated them into his plans, and they were being killed, too, but he had not anticipated that blind passionate loving of them and fear for them that entered his brother's eyes at the moment of death. And he had forgotten that Wen didn't like churches, except for building them. Wenceslas would never have sought sanctuary in a mere church but only, as always before, beneath the open sky. There was only one fugitive being denied sanctuary at this locked church door today. Bo could hear him, sobbing, begging for mercy, but just now could not quite remember what that person's name was.

POSTSCRIPT

Boleslav ruled Bohemia until 967. His long and prosperous reign saw the addition of Moravia, Slovakia, and Silesia to his domains and the extension of Christianity into these formerly pagan lands. In 955, he helped defeat the Magyars in a battle that secured relative peace in the area for generations. His son, too, became a mighty king. One might say that Boleslav reaped every blessing that his brother had wished on him.

It seems a bit unfair, therefore, that Boleslav should still be called, a millenium after his death, by the name he was given in life by the troublemakers, priests, and radicals who occupied the far peripheries of his reign. Boleslav the Cruel was how they styled him, and Boleslav the Cruel he remains.

In our own harsh and unromantic days, one worries about any people who, like the Czechs, continue to honor as their patron one of the Wenceslases of this world rather than pinning their hopes on a Boleslav. "Vaclav" is the Czech equivalent of "Wenceslas," so Vaclav Havel, hero of the Czech liberation, has this misfit adolescent as his name saint. These Czechs seem to keep on surviving though, despite the best efforts of their surrounding enemies. Maybe Wenceslas does have some magic left even for our times.

Nonetheless, the Czechs would be the first to advise you that, should the day ever dawn that whatever gestapo momentarily in power knocks on your door and tells you that the Wenceslas carol has been condemned as antisocial, you should be very polite. I would suggest singing instead the following verse about Boleslav. Whoever these gestapo are in your day, I can guarantee you they will approve of Boleslav if you explain him quite carefully to them. If this first verse works, feel free to devise a few more for yourself, so long as they remind you, as you sing them, never ever to forget the dear old perennially confusing lines of the original.

> Cruel King Boleslav spoke out
> Assassination evening,
> Told the nobles round about
> That he was going to be King,
> Told them he'd restore the draft
> And make Bohemia mighty,
> Called social justice just plain daft;
> Said Christians were too flighty.

One further footnote about Saint Agnes's Fountain: The Czech Saint Agnes was actually a descendent of Wenceslas who, several hundred years after his death, found in Saint Francis and Saint Clare the natural spiritual companionship that Wenceslas had been born too soon to attain. (Agnes jilted an emperor to become a nun, but that is another story.) One might choose to dismiss this connection as an error of the Victorian lyricist, but I prefer to believe that somehow the peasants in her great-grand-ancestor's day knew already that there would someday have to be an Agnes and named their fountain after this unborn heir of their beloved King, understanding already that his fate would have no boundaries in time.

MAIDS

FRANCIS AND CLARE

THE FIRST CHRISTMAS
PAGEANT

I will make you brooches and toys for your delight,
Of bird-song at morning and star-shine at night.
I will make a palace fit for you and me,
Of green days in forests and blue days at sea.

—ROBERT LOUIS STEVENSON, *The Collected Poems*

FRANCIS AND CLARE

SAINT FRANCIS WAS BORN IN ASSISI, Italy, over 800 years ago, in 1181 or 1182. In 1224, the stigmata of the crucifixion appeared on his body; that event is celebrated on September 17. He died on October 3, 1226, and is remembered on October 4. The bare facts sound so remotely long ago, and neither saints nor stigmata provide the thrill they once did. Yet, phrases from the poems of Francis keep cropping up today: "Lord, make me an instrument of your peace," "Brother Sun, Sister Moon," "our Lady Poverty." Bits of the poetry that he lived have remained stuck, too, in our consciousness. One imagines him setting off for battle in awkward new armor on one of his failed slapstick attempts to become an ordinary military knight-errant, rather than the master of mystical chivalry that God had destined him to be. We can envision the moment when suddenly he succeeded in fighting back his terror and ran up to the leper he has seen on the road and kissed him.

The wonder of Francis is that he knew he was doing it for himself more than for the leper. So many of us don't see that. Another time, a bishop chastised Francis for taking his father's money to rebuild the crumbled church at San Damiano. "The clothes I wear are his also," said Francis, and stripped them—all of them—from his body in front of the Bishop and all his court. One always feels that Francis earned, with infinite thought and sweat, every particle of every miracle he ever wrought. When the other brothers labeled a certain leper as impossible to deal with, Francis himself took over the case. Immediately, the patient's incessant moaning and complaining ceased. "What did you do?" asked the brothers. "I just do whatever he asks me to do," said Francis, omitting to mention the superhuman sensitivity and the round-the-clock drudgery needed for this simple commitment. And the leper was made whole.

Even on his deathbed, Francis was at it still, with the perfect gesture, the authentic attitude. When he knew his Sister Death was near, he asked the brothers to place his naked body on the bare ground and leave him alone there to die. He suggested they might take a small walk.

For those who mistakenly believe fame to be a uniquely modern curse, the life of Francis is instructive. By the time he was thirty-four, five thousand Franciscans were turning up for chapter meetings, more than could be entertained comfortably even at a picnic. "Would that there were fewer Friars Minor," said Francis, "and that the world should so rarely see one as to wonder at their fewness."

Francis was a radical. One thinks of the time when he returned from a journey to find a beautiful new roof crowning his church. He leapt up to the top of it and began throwing down the expensive tiles, smashing them one by one. And there are the tales of how, when Francis came to visit one of his own friaries, he was turned away as too filthy and too diseased even for a beggar. All this radical love for Lady Poverty took the church and the world rather by surprise. It wasn't until after his death that these predictable institutions recovered enough to mount a persecution of those radical spirituals among the Franciscans who demanded absolute poverty. Within one hundred years of Francis's death, this radical group ceased to exist.

Saint Clare was born in Assisi about 1193. She met Francis when she was eighteen. On the night of Palm Sunday in 1212, she ran away from home with the assistance of a key to the city walls that had been slipped to her by one of the brothers. She made her way to the chapel of Our Lady of the Angels at the Portiuncula, where Francis and the brothers lived. Francis himself hacked off her hair that night and accepted her into the order. It is said that, when her relatives came to take her back home where she belonged, Clare grabbed onto the altar with such strength that the altar cloths were pulled down in the ensuing tug of war. Clare herself did not budge from the altar she had chosen. She founded the Poor Clares and served as their abbess for forty years. Years later, a Saracen invasion attempted to budge her from her convent, again with a notable lack of success. Clare died on August 11, 1253, at age sixty. Her day is celebrated on August 12. Like Francis, Clare was canonized by popular acclaim within a few years of her death.

THE FIRST
CHRISTMAS PAGEANT

Clare had had them put her great carved desk in the convent's kitchen. She remembered how pained Francis had looked. She wondered if he disliked the desk because it reminded him of her family and how they raged when they believed that Francis had kidnapped her to bring her to his convent. She smiled as she remembered her uncle thundering in with his soldiers. Francis had utterly failed to see the logic of his outrage and her poor uncle had left confused. No, Francis had never noticed her family enough to dislike them. He disapproved of the desk because it would not fit through the eye of a needle. But her uncle had needed to bring her something. Uncle still understood nothing, except that he and Francis both loved her. Had she persisted in saying no, everyone would have thought her an ungrateful fool. And she needed the desk. There in the kitchen she could keep an eye on the cooking pot and a nose on the bread and greet the sisters as they came in the back door with quail's eggs or fresh raspberries. She could do all these things and at the same time write letters to the Pope. Since Francis had left, there had been need for many such letters. The Pope had little idea of what Francis was about, and Clare had little better. Fine time for Francis to take a handful of brothers and disappear, as always, for months on end.

Clare realized suddenly what had been distracting her and leading her down these musty mental labyrinths: it was the smell of smoke. That was what made her finally look up and see him. It was not the soup burning after all, just that strange lightning that always leapt between him and her. That was how people in the neighborhood could tell that Francis was back from a journey. They came running to see if the forest was on fire, and there would be Francis standing awkwardly in Clare's doorway, making conversation and lightning.

Clare ran to kiss her cousin Rufino. Both he and Francis looked awful, she thought, and there was something wrong with Francis's eye. It was red and streaming. He turned, and she saw that the other eye was sealed over by a white scar. No more flecks of green irony. This time, the farmers reported later, the streak of jagged lightning flashed out from Clare.

"I am a much more convincing beggar now," Francis said, "and I see better, too, especially with this white eye. It reduces everything to light. I am sure our eyes interfere with what God means for us to see. And I have brought you a present."

He brought one dove out of each pocket and the pair flew up into the rafters of the chapter house where they began to murmur to each other.

"These two are singers," he said. "If you start singing they'll fly right to your shoulder and hum along."

Changing the subject. It would take days to get the story and most of the reality would have to come from Rufino. She struggled back to essentials. "The trip. Where did you go? Where have you been all these months?"

"You know, I noticed this time that all these pilgrimages are the same trip. It doesn't matter where we go," said Francis. "It doesn't matter what language the people are speaking. The same things happen to us every single time. When we crossed the crusaders' lines to go see the Sultan, our soldiers thought we were spies and beat us with clubs. Then we came to the Sultan's soldiers who beat us with clubs, too, but it was all the same thing, and the soldiers themselves might all have been natives of Assisi. They smelled just the same as the soldiers who club us here and they were just as afraid of us. The Sultan says he won't stop fighting."

Clare sighed. Francis's idea about the Crusades was that all would be well if he could just explain to the Moslems why he in particular, and Christianity in general, so desperately required the territory between Bethlehem and Jerusalem. He was sure that once they understood why the Christians were killing them, the Moslems would most graciously and courteously withdraw. Clare would have to find out from Rufino what had really happened.

"Francis, have they told you about the new rules? What the Pope is saying is essentially 'No exceptions for Francis!' He wants us to fast on Fridays, and own land and monasteries and keep to schedules just as they do in all the other orders. Tomorrow is Christmas Eve, but it's a Friday, too. The whole valley keeps bringing us food and drink, but I haven't been able to decide what to do about anything. I guess I was waiting for you. I worry that we'll end up letting all this food rot. All I know is that they're all watching us now in Rome, waiting for a mistake, and whatever we do will be taken as a mistake. The pope doesn't understand beggars in the first place, and he cannot really comprehend that begging is how we live. He says that if we would only consent to use money like everyone else, all our problems would be solved."

Francis thought. "Well, we always fast in Advent anyway. Joseph and Mary had no food on that journey and no one in Bethlehem would give them a crust. Poor holy family, they were worse beggars even than I. Why not fast on Christmas Eve, too? Why not Christmas Day? Now the angels came and brought the shepherds to see the babe, but angels don't eat and what food could the shepherds have shared? Hard bread and goat's milk, same as our shepherds in winter. Hallelujah, Clare, I believe, if we think this through, we can find a way to fast 'til Epiphany! The three kings would have fed them of course, but before that, they could not have had a decent meal for days. Not in Bethlehem with that crew of money-grubbers. It's so clear. A good long fast for Christmas, twelve days until Epiphany...I wonder why I never thought of it before?"

"Stop, stop," said Clare, "The Pope told me that one reason he wants us to fast on Fridays is so that he can put some limit on these massive fasting projects of yours. You would have us fasting the whole year through. This idea of a two-week fast has cheered you well enough, but what am I going to do with all this food?"

A man and his wife brought a fresh-killed pig to the back door and Francis helped them to tie its back legs to a rafter.

"That will never last 'til Epiphany," said Clare.

"What we need is a way," mused Francis, "to get the poor people together so they can eat what the rich people are bringing to us while we fast.

"There is a cave about ten miles from here. It is near a small village where the people are greedy and spiteful. The peasants keep cattle in the cave. If you dressed as Mary, and I as Joseph, we could make a procession to the cave carrying our feast in carts and barrows. All the sisters and brothers will follow singing. The poor will smell the food and follow us. The rich will hear the singing and bring more food. The money-grubbing villagers will come and find salvation. You and I will fast not just to follow the Pope's rule, but to follow in the footsteps of Good Joseph and the Blessed Virgin, sharing in the clear, hard joy that Christmas brought to them. Our little brothers and sisters will see that and fast joyfully with us, building fires and cooking food so that rich and poor can feast together on the mountainside..."

Clare began to laugh. "Have you noticed, Francis, that every one of our struggles, and every one of our journeys comes to rest on the grass in a picnic? Picnics are mostly what we do in this order."

"I had a picnic with the Sultan, too," said Francis, "but it didn't help. I wonder why no one has ever thought of a Christmas picnic before? The picnic part is lovely, but, Clare, have you considered the animals? Think of all the animals we can bring! Perhaps even the humming doves, to help the brothers sing. Why we'll feast all the birds along the way, strewing bread crumbs until the heavens are full of singing just as when the angels sang His coming."

Birds always did follow Francis, bread crumbs or no, and he loved to preach to them. This, in fact, is the origin of an old saying you may have heard and wondered about. One day, Francis was trying out a sermon on the brothers. Everybody hated it; they thought it was the worst sermon they had ever heard. Francis shrugged. "Well," he said, "I guess that one will have to be for the birds."

"I must go teach those doves the Gloria," he said now. "And remember that clever little donkey I gave you? The one who bows three times and makes the sign of the cross with his hoof in the sand? He does it after the amens, no? And do you still have that pair of sheep that followed me home Easter a year ago? You haven't eaten them? Not overly bright, those two, but they did learn to nod their heads in rhythm to the Our Father. They just looked so bored when they did it that we all lost our places laughing. I wonder if I could teach them to come in with the shepherds and bow down before the Christ Child? They are stupid, but I believe that, if I explain the situation to them fully...that we've nobody else qualified to play the sheep...I believe they would pitch in and try their best."

He was off and running. Clare called after him, "With all this, Francis, don't you think we'll need permission from the Pope?"

Francis turned his blind eye to her. "No. He'll love it. It's so practical. The only time the Pope gets upset with me is when I'm not practical. That's how he begins all his letters, 'Francis, please be practical.' It's a lovely meditation for me. A penance, actually, because I never realized how difficult it would be, being practical. How much fasting and begging and picnicking it involves. There are so many animals one must meet and engage as helpers and so many things to give away. By the way, I know a family near the cave in sore need of firewood. They could use that desk of yours, and, if we carry it, in the procession, we can fill the drawers with nuts and berries. The best thing about being practical is that everything works out so thoroughly that way. There is no weight left on the conscience."

He was turning to go to the barns now, to find the sheep. Clare did what she always did when he went away. She closed her eyes and said in her mind something that might have sounded out loud a little like this: "Before you perhaps forever go away again as always before, I perhaps could never say your pain is with me always before your eyes gone grey and yearning after roads past all returning, we'll say…" Out loud she said "goodbye" and then opened her eyes to find Francis safely vanished. Rufino was there still, but nonetheless it crossed her mind that maybe Francis had not been there at all this time really, maybe he had never even existed except as her own private invention.

"How ill is he?" Clare asked Rufino.

"Three weeks from the last crazy fever. He was fighting off rats. That's how I knew he was hallucinating. If they had been real rats he would have taught them the Hail Mary. The eye business has fever with it too. The children had it there in the Holy Land. He would seek out the blind little ones so he could tell them how the birds look and the flowers."

"How much was he tortured?"

"The Sultan dared not lay a hand on him. As I understand, the Sultan has his own holy madmen and they must never be harmed. Francis played with the fires for the Sultan, but you know the flames are his brothers and never burn him."

Francis came running back holding a piece of firewood. "This is for the Christ Child," he said. They looked at each other and began to laugh and, as they did so, holding the lump of firewood in both their hands, it began to smell of burning. They carved it into a baby, the two of them, as easily as if it had been made of butter.

That is how on that Christmas morning in 1220, Clare came to be sitting hungry in some rotting hay on the floor of a cave in a mountain in the company of two bowing sheep, a trained donkey, a wooden doll, a rooster that had been taught to crow Hallelujahs, innumerable candles and singing birds, countless brothers and sisters, and a strange half-blind man whom she had always loved.

The rain had turned to snow, and the money-grubbing villagers were charging the price of a ruby for a bit of roof. Everyone was cold and miserable. Francis had done it again, had taken an ordinary Friday Christmas Eve and turned it into something far worse, something very like a crucifixion.

Francis had been smiling at the wooden doll all night in that shining way that meant he was praying. At last he reached out his arms to the wooden babe, as if he had just been granted permission. As he picked it up, the doll became, in his arms, a living baby; it cried a bit. Clare reached for it and it became wood again. Then it was a baby again; then wood. Back and forth it changed, until Clare wasn't sure she could tell the difference any more or even if there were a difference.

Francis was so happy that Clare, too, began to laugh. He did love these miracles with all his soul. That was why they kept on happening to him because he was the only one who thoroughly appreciated them. Now as they laughed the lightning began again to sparkle between them, not jagged now, but soft round pulses of light, surrounding them like a halo. The peasants, who saw it so much more clearly than either Francis or Clare, edged closer to warm their hands at the fire those two made.

POSTSCRIPT

In fact, the Pope did not give permission for Francis's Christmas crèche until 1223, and history recounts that the first Christmas pageant took place in that year. However, those of us who know Francis well cannot believe that he really waited for permission. Thus, I have pushed the date of the story's creche back a few years. His visit to the Sultan took place in 1219–1220, and he did return ill and on the verge of blindness. I again have taken liberties, in diagnosing malaria and trachoma. The quarrels with the Pope, the picnics, the lightning with Clare, Clare's letter writing, the doves, the miracle of the quickening Jesus doll—all are part of the history and legend of Saint Francis.

There is another Francis-and-Clare story that I cannot resist telling even though its only relevance is that it, too, happened one Christmas. Saint Clare, you may have heard, is the patron saint of television, and this is why: One Christmas, when she was an old lady and Francis was long since dead, consumed by the fires of pain that were his brothers, Clare woke too ill to go to mass. She tried with all her might to get out of bed, but her body would not do it. Francis could always make his spirit take his body where it needed to be, but he was himself; she was only Clare. Finally, her sisters left without her. They returned, full of regrets that she had missed such a beautiful Christmas service. "Don't worry," said Clare. "I saw it all. It was not the same as being in my own chair. The angle was different. I saw everything as if from a high point, like the choir loft, but as if I were very close to it all as well. Odd, but I did see and hear the entire service in every detail. Was I flying, I wonder? Flying or, more likely perhaps, dying? Oh, if only Francis were here...this is exactly the kind of miracle that would make him laugh all day."

GILLES DE RAIS
AND JOAN OF ARC

LITTLE KEY, SET ME FREE

To Joan and her contemporaries we should appear as a drove of Gadarene swine, possessed by all the unclean spirits cast out by the faith and civilization of the Middle Ages and running violently down a steep place into a hell of high explosives.

—GEORGE BERNARD SHAW,
From the introduction to *Saint Joan*

I say that we are wound with mercy round and round—as if with air.

—GERARD MANLEY HOPKINS,
The Collected Poems

GILLES DE RAIS AND JOAN OF ARC

IN A DRUGSTORE I BOUGHT A TRUE-CRIME novel for its lurid cover, and that was my introduction to the Baron Gilles de Rais, who in turn introduced me to his friend and former commanding officer, Joan of Arc. Gilles de Rais was born in 1404. He was one of the richest men in France when, in his early twenties, he was assigned by the Dauphin (the Crown Prince of France) to keep guard over Joan of Arc. Gilles saved Joan's life on at least three occasions and later wrote a miracle play about her, which was performed every year at Orléans in gratitude to her for delivering the city from the hands of its enemy.

Gilles was just the first of many biographers to be fascinated by Joan of Arc. Joan was born either in 1412 or 1413. No one is sure which year is correct, because in the beginning it did not seem worthwhile to be precise about the life of a mere daughter and a peasant at that. In January of 1429, Joan left her home village of Domrémy to find the Dauphin. She planned to help him drive back the English invaders, so he could be crowned King. Joan said that saints Michael, Catherine, and Margaret had told her to do this.

The deepest mystery about Joan is that she did exactly what she set out to do. By April, she had convinced the King and parliament to grant her horses, armor, and troops. By May, she had startled the English into raising the siege of Orléans. On July 17, after four more spectacular military victories, Joan rode her warhorse into the Cathedral at Reims to watch the coronation of King Charles VII.

However, the next spring, on May 23, 1430, Joan was taken prisoner in battle. Her English captors arranged a witchcraft trial by the Inquisition which was neither quite fair nor terribly polite. One of the major charges against her was that she wore men's clothing. She tried to explain that she worked as a soldier, so she wore what soldiers wore. The trial dragged on until May 30, 1431, when Joan was burned at the stake, a convicted heretic. As George Bernard Shaw has noted, the men around Joan made sure she never got out of her teens. We can only imagine what she would have been like had she lived to become a grown-up.

Twenty years after her death, Charles VII encouraged the Inquisition to reopen Joan's case, and the guilty verdict was overturned. Some believe this was bit late in the day for Charles to leap to the rescue of the girl who, in his own darkest days, had been his fiercest champion.

There are, of course, many more stories about Joan, more than any one person could possibly tell. One childhood friend told the inquisitors about a day long before, when, as she was running through a field, Joan had caught her hand, and together they had run so hard that it had seemed their feet left the ground. In retrospect, she thought that perhaps she and Joan had been flying together that day, hand in hand. At the time it had not seemed to matter much whether it was flying that had happened to them or merely some other wonderful something. And even if they had been truly flying, did that mean Joan was a witch? Or did it mean she was a saint? Or was Joan just that kind of a girl? The kind who makes you feel like you're flying?

Gilles de Rais was deeply troubled when he heard the news of Joan's capture. Shortly after Joan's execution, the Baron swore vengeance on the English and at the Battle of Lagny, he fought them like a maniac. The many English prisoners taken by the Baron on that day were either killed outright or tortured to death in dungeons.

By 1435, the Baron was in deep financial trouble, largely because of his extravagance in support of his private army and of the arts (especially his famous boys' choir). Gilles's relatives and potential heirs convinced the King to bar Gilles de Rais from selling any more of his numerous lands and castles. In desperation the Baron turned to an alchemist, François Prelati, who promised to make gold from coal with the aid of incense, a magnet stone, the devil, and, optionally, the eyes and heart of a little child.

This story is set in 1439, at Christmastime, eight years after Joan's trial and execution and in the thirty-sixth year of the life of the Baron, Gilles de Rais.

LITTLE KEY, SET ME FREE

Once upon a time there was a girl who sneaked with her cousin over the roofs and into the great castle of La Suze in Nantes to see the Advent feast laid on there by the Baron, Gilles de Rais. The two children saw from the roof into the courtyard where leaf-bare trees were now painted blue with gold and silvery things hanging on ribbons from the branches, things like bells and a trumpet and a raven in a gilded cage who ruffled his wings now and again and chanted "Come to me, gentle child." They saw blooming rosebushes and orange trees in pots and, in the porticoes, tables laid with blue cloths and roasted lambs and large pots of roasted apples. They saw the choir boys from the Chapel of the Holy Innocents caped in gold and crimson over blue, with bells, and striped sleeves swooping nearly to the ground.

Then toward sundown the girl's cousin crept down from the roof to see more. There was a wooden trunk in the courtyard, intricately carved. Sometimes when one of the choirboys passed he would reach in and bring out something wonderful. There were swords and tiny soldiers and catapults and wooden animals—bears and horses, unicorns and satyrs and a dragon whose tail circled and circled around him. They were all painted blue, these pretty animals, and both children longed to touch them.

After that it got very dark and the cousin was still not back and it started to rain and rain and when the bells struck twelve in the Chapel of the Holy Innocents the girl was too afraid to wait any longer and crept down herself into the courtyard, still torchlit and crowded with children and jugglers and mummers and clowns. Her body ached from the strain of the worrying and from trying to stay invisible and her beating heart was driving her to find her cousin as fast as she could. Fast, fast, fast, said her heart but when she found herself close to that large carved box, the one with the pretty things, she stopped. Her cousin had probably gotten his look inside already, and maybe even taken something out and was playing with it now somewhere and that was why he had forgotten her. She knelt down before it and just as she got it unlatched and was easing the lid up enough to see inside, an icy vise of bony, disapproving fingers closed around her neck and she was lifted high into the air.

She awoke naked in a fragrant golden candlelit bath as a witch, who was the only other person there, was pouring more scalding hot water down on top of her. The girl screamed and explained and protested and threatened while the witch scrubbed her body until it hurt. Once those strong cruel fingers started in on the back of her neck the girl knew for sure it was the witch who had grabbed her and brought her here. It took longer for the girl to realize that the witch was deaf, stark stone deaf, and had heard nothing of all the girl's pleading.

The witch was talking, too, muttering that this one was a girl, after all, and that might anger the master. He liked little boys the best, although one never could be sure what would take his fancy. The witch laughed.

The old witch dressed the girl in one of the crimson and gold and blue choir robes and placed a tiny golden key in her hand. "Take this key and give it to the master. He's the one with the blue beard. Address him respectfully with all his titles: Gilles de Rais, Baron, Marshal of France, Lord of Champtoce, and Tiffauges, of Machecoul, of Saint Etienne de le Mer Morts, of Pornic and of Vue. Tell him you are at his service and give him this key." Then the witch pushed the girl back out into the courtyard and followed her warily across it until the girl came under the black eyes of a huge man in black whose neck was hung with golden chains and whose every finger sparkled with jewels. His blue beard looked very strange because he had not bothered to dye his hair to match. The girl was still looking for her cousin but she remembered to say the words in proper order.

The Baron took the key and with his other hand lifted her face into the light. To his servant, he said, "Look at this beautiful little head, Poitou. Perhaps you would do better to wait until morning to collect that box I mentioned—the box for the moat at Champtoce. I plan to add a little something more to it before morning." They laughed.

The Baron took the girl's hand and chatted in the friendliest possible way with her as he led her up an outer staircase from the courtyard and down a roofed corridor and inside through another longer darker corridor and through another door and up a narrow winding staircase that ended at a shining brass door that even a child would have to crouch to get through.

The Baron was saying the names of battles and of armor and breeds of warhorses and types of swords. He was going to show her his collection of swords or something like that. It was hard to pay much attention. The girl was still keeping an eye out for her cousin. Also, she thought maybe the Baron was boasting. She had always had trouble paying attention when someone was boasting.

Two things she noticed very clearly, though: first, that the Baron locked the small bright door behind him and hung the tiny key on its chain around his neck, and second, that one of the swords on the wall, a very old silvery one, seemed to light up as the Baron lit the candles around the room. The sword was carved with symbols from handle to blade-tip, spidery delicate things that might have been writing or might have been pictures. The girl thought that sword was the only real thing in that room.

The Baron brought it down for her and told her its story.

"That is the sword of Joan of Arc. Everyone knows the story of her magic sword, but no other living person knows where it rests. That first day they met, Joan told the Dauphin to send men to search behind the altar at the Shrine of Saint Catherine of Fierbois. I led that noble party. We dug in the place the Maid had told us and found this ancient sword. Before that, the Dauphin had not believed Joan had the power to make him King of France. It was the sword that made him believe. With this sword Joan raised the siege of Orléans. I was with her at Orléans and saved her life. It was I who held off the enemy as she pulled out the arrow that had pierced her neck. It was a true miracle that I witnessed that day. Not one drop of blood came from that wound. Two times more I saved her life in battle. I was her only true friend, the only man in France who recognized her importance. I alone had the courage to ride to rescue her after the English imprisoned her. She is the only woman I ever loved. She is the only human being I've ever met worthy enough to see past all this blue beard of mine to the noble suffering soul inside. Nobody else has ever loved me."

He was crying now and kissing the sword. There was more, but the girl was having trouble paying attention again. She had the feeling that all these things had been said many, many times before. She was amazed to see real tears dripping through his bejewelled fingers as he sobbed his fake sobs and she was about to say that it seemed to her the witch loved him, when suddenly there came a knocking and a shouting at the little brass door.

The Baron drew himself up, pale with rage and trembling a little, and screamed, "I have told you, Poitou, never ever to interrupt me in this room."

"But, Master," quailed the voice from behind the door, "it's the Maid, Joan. Joan of Arc has returned. She just entered the courtyard with all her retinue."

Again the Baron changed entirely. Now he trembled with stark fear as he sank once more onto the stool. "I did it," he muttered. "I am the one who called her back from the dead. Last night when the Magician made the enchanted circle, he set the lumps of coal in the center of the ring to be changed into gold. He told us all to call on the names of Satan, Belial, and Beelzebub, but something terrible happened to me. At the moment I was to say the holy names, it was as if a demon seized control of my tongue. 'Joan of Arc,' I shouted, all against my will, 'Joan of Arc.' And now she has come."

Wearily, he pulled himself together to leave. At the door, his rage came back for an instant. "Stay here you little wretch. If you move so much as one muscle before I get back, I'll cut out both your eyes."

This is how it happened that the girl was left alone to explore that curious tower room. She noticed now that a heavy blue curtain blocked off the back part of the chamber. The walls were blue, too, and the ceiling. She saw, too, a small puddle seeping toward her across the blue floor from the other side of the curtain.

The other side of that curtain seemed very far away from the candles and very dark. The first thing the girl saw was the glint of a dozen knives hanging on the wall. Not swords here, but the sort of knives the butcher used. There was a table, too, like the butcher's table, and on that table was a human skull and onto the skull hop-hopping (suddenly, so that the girl jumped back) came a fat, knobbly toad.

In the far corner, a noose dangled from the ceiling. Beyond the noose there were shelves, and on the shelves, lined up neatly in rows, like a collection, started out at her the chopped-off heads of boys—more of them than she could count or even really see except she could not help seeing the last head on the last row, which she recognized at once, as she had been looking and looking for it ever since sundown.

The girl saw, too, that the puddle was coming from a large trunk and she knew without looking further, what was in that box—the rest of her cousin.

The girl backed slowly away. The candles flickered and suddenly blew out, whoosh! Then, clang! she backed into one of the suits of armor.

The girl whirled around into unexpected light. The armor seemed to be shining, reflecting the light of some sun that she could not see. The girl's eyes had to adjust before she could recognize the Maid Joan. Then her heart sank because she thought the Baron must be close behind.

"Don't worry," said Joan of Arc, "the Baron is still closeted somewhere with my impostor. She'll keep him tied up for hours. I believe he is the only person in France still capable of being fooled by that woman. Her real name is Jeanne des Armoises. My brothers found her in Italy. She really believes she is me. My brothers do it for the money. They lead her about France and collect money ostensibly for honors to Joan of Arc and for wars against the English, both equally and regrettably unlikely in this modern world."

"The Baron said he brought you back, but I knew you were dead," said the girl.

"He lies so much," said Joan. "He loses track, but even normal people refuse sometimes to believe I am dead. What a ridiculous mistake! How could someone like me survive in France except burnt to cinders? All but my heart, which even the flames could not touch, and my soul, which belongs to my liege Lord. Not the poor pompous Dauphin any longer, thank goodness, but a Lord made more to my measure. I was sent here in fact on my Lord's business. It's He who requires the soul of this Baron, and I have come to collect it."

The girl said nothing but wondered bitterly whatever a fine Lord *could* want with such a slimy soul as the Baron's.

"I ask myself the same question," said Joan. "I don't know, either. I still wonder what He wanted with my soul. I had some need of it myself, was using it in fact at the very moment He called for it. This Baron, though, is the vilest job I've ever been sent to do. Do you know how the Baron got my sword? One day back when we were all soldiering together, Poitou tried to run away. In those days, Poitou served the Baron as page. He had good reason to run, too; Poitou was the Baron's first and favorite victim. I saw the Baron screaming and choking the boy, and dashed in to help. Somehow in the fray, I threw down my sword. I didn't want to sully it on a thing like Gilles de Rais. Fingernails and teeth seemed weapons more suited to his dignity. He never gave it back. Just as well. If I'd had a sword in my hand by the end of that fight I would have killed him straight out, and I made it a point never to use that sword for killing. There are more beautiful ways to win.

"My favorite battle was the one at Orléans when we lined up in front of the English and they lined up in front of us and we stared at each other for two hours. We looked at them so carefully that after a while they could not bear to be seen that clearly any more. One by one those English knights, sheepish and embarrassed, turned their horses round and walked away. Someday, somehow, that is the thing I will do to the Baron, and then I will have his soul in the palm of my hand."

"I have looked at him very carefully," said the girl, "but I don't think that will stop him killing me." Her voice was sounding surprisingly small. "He wants to cut off my head and put it in his collection. He said I have the finest head he's found." Very slowly, the girl noticed that her legs were giving way, leaving her dumped onto the floor in a small limp heap.

Joan of Arc pointed to the door, and the light from her armor illuminated the small gold key that the Baron, in his terror, had left in the lock on the inside of that door, which was drifting open now by just the faintest, feeblest and most encouraging of cracks. For a heartbeat or two, the girl felt there might be some hope of escape.

"It's no good," she said. "I can't make myself move. I'm too scared."

"Do you know what I do when I'm afraid?" said Joan. "I pray. I find it takes my mind off unnecessary details. Also, if you can say out loud exactly what you feel and what you need then you've already solved so many of your problems. It's even better really to pray in poems because then you have to think through the rhymes and that takes your mind off everything."

At that moment the girl had not the slightest interest in Joan of Arc's prayer poems. She had had about all the saintliness she could stand. "If you really wanted to help, you would open that door yourself and get me out of here."

Joan seemed not to notice this outburst, as she was already experimenting with rhymes, humming them to herself with her gaze unfocussed onto something in the general direction of the blue ceiling.

Little key, set me free.

Help him fail to chop up me.

Little key, can't you see?

Only I can rescue me.

Lord, make courage grow in me,

And help me turn this blasted key.

Some must watch and some must pray.

Watchers' heads end on a tray,

Sped there by their own delay.

I'm not too scared to run away,

And though I faint and fret and fray,

Someday I'll get you, Gilles de Rais.

Something about the rhyme grated so and the whole approach seemed so utterly childish, that the girl, out of sheer irritation, pulled herself to her feet and walked to the door. It was not until her hand touched the tiny key that she realized what she was doing, and began to shake and tremble again so badly that she knocked the key onto the floor and right into the pool of blood, which had now spread and crept even further along the tower floor.

Joan decided it was time to use her best magic. This girl had really lost her nerve and, left to her own devices, would still be leaning whitely against the wall staring down at that bloody key when the Baron returned. Joan took up her sword from the blue stool where the Baron had dropped it. "Take this," she said. "It will give you strength."

At first the girl simply held the heavy silvery sword and stared hard at it. Then, all of a sudden, she tossed the sword back to Joan, picked up the key from the bloody blue floor, opened the little door, closed and locked it carefully, put the key around her neck, and ran and ran and ran.

The courtyard was deserted except for a thin gray priest sitting on that enormous toy box under the blue trees. He seemed to be counting the stars. "I beg your pardon, young man," he said to the girl. "I'm the new bishop here. Can you tell me if the choir's Christmas concert has been canceled? I've been waiting for hours, but it's as though this castle were enchanted. I haven't seen a soul in all this time." The girl opened her mouth but no sounds came out. The best she could do was to grab the bloody key, pull it off her neck and hand it to the Bishop. Generous and simply helpful as he always was, the Bishop brought out his large white embroidered bishop's handkerchief and began wiping the blood off the key. He cleaned and polished it quite thoroughly. However, when he turned the key over to inspect it before handing it back, he saw that somehow he had missed all the spots on the other side.

Twenty minutes later, the Bishop was still patiently polishing first one side and then the other of that persistently bloody key. The girl had caught her breath and was describing in detail the tower room. "Come with me now," she pleaded. "I can show you the severed heads. I have given you the key to all the evidence you'll need. I know where the bodies are buried. With my help you can make the Baron stop."

Joan, still holding her sword, watched the scene from the steps. Joan had watched the faces of many men talking to women, weighing against the sweet certainty of ultimate success the social consequences of acquiring an embarrassing female ally. She sighed happily and turned to climb back up the stairs. It was obvious that the girl would win, although the Bishop probably would not know it for days, if ever.

Joan gave a friendly kiss to her sword's fine hilt. "These mortals fall for you every time," she said. "My dear boastful Dauphin always loved you, too, and his visions of your magic. Even now, they tell me that old King Charles is scouring all France, still trying to find this scrap of tarnished silver and still hoping to regain his lost courage. He doesn't know that it's still inside him, if only he would look there."

POSTSCRIPT

Joan of Arc's sword was never found. This may be why the world has not improved much in all these years.

Jeanne des Armoises finally got tired of touring France in the guise of Joan of Arc and went back home to take care of her children.

Jean de Malestroit, Bishop of Nantes, organized the trial of Gilles de Rais. The sane, matter-of-fact tone of that trial and its almost modern use of rules of evidence stand in marked contrast to the bullying and name-calling which were the principal weapons used against Joan when she was tried.

Gilles de Rais was charged with the murders of 208 children who had been reported missing by neighboring families. Forty bodies were found buried in the moat at Champtoce and forty skulls at the Castle of Machecoul. Almost all of the children on the list were boys between the ages of eight and twelve. The Bishop was greatly assisted in his investigation by one girl who had been mistaken by the Baron for a boy because of her dress, but then released. A short seventeen-year-old boy had also been released when the Baron saw how old he was. Most of the vanished females on the victim list were pregnant women. I will not even hazard a guess at the uses Gilles de Rais made of them.

The boys on the list had begun to disappear in 1432, but the numbers had increased year by year. By 1440, the Baron had enlisted his noble friends as assistants in massive holiday hunts for boys. They would swoop down on every boy they saw on the road, grab them up onto their saddles, and ride home to lock them up in the tower room. The grown-up hunters thought this was great fun. They said at the trial that they could not be blamed for helping because they never knew what happened to the children after capture. Poitou, the page, and Perrine Martin, the witch, were tried with the Baron and were executed with him on October 26, 1440.

Again, in contrast to Joan, who was burned alive, the Baron was granted the privilege of being strangled to death before his body was burned at the stake. This was granted because of the Baron's good Christian attitude and his great repentance for his sinful deeds. Joan had declined to repent or regret a thing.

In a pious speech before his execution, the Baron said that he had gone bad because his guardians had not beaten him hard enough or often enough. He urged mothers everywhere to beat their children without mercy. In memory of the dreadful deeds of Gilles de Rais. To this day, on the Halloweenish anniversary of the Baron's death, mothers in that part of France still whip each of their children methodically. If a child has been especially bad that year, the mother may take the child, on that spooky late October day, to the creepy ruins of the castle at Machecoul so the child can have the beating in the midst of the ghosts of all the children murdered there. All of this goes to show that Gilles de Rais was very powerful when it came to hurting kids and is still managing to do it five hundred years after his death.

Did Joan get his soul in the end? Or did Lucifer? Or did both of them lose interest in that soul while listening to the endless gruesome details of the Baron's confession? He told how he violated the little bodies of his victims while he was strangling and beheading them and again after they were dead. He told many other things which no doubt made him feel better, but which made everyone else feel worse.

You may have noticed that this story is a lot like *Bluebeard,* that scary tale in which a beautiful new wife finds the bodies of her husband's former wives in a mysterious, locked room. That is because Gilles de Rais was the real-life model for Bluebeard. In George Bernard Shaw's play *Saint Joan,* the actor who plays the Baron must wear a blue beard. I have always wondered why the blue beard is such a good clue in that story. I think it's because when someone does something very weird and ugly, it is not enough just to be polite and say nothing. Even if the person is old and rich and respectable, you have to ask why. Maybe they have a good reason, or maybe the "blue beard" means they don't respect what you respect, and if that's what's going on, you cannot let yourself trust them, not even an inch.

The bloody key comes from that story, too. In the old story it gets the girl into a lot of trouble because Bluebeard realizes that to have gotten blood on the key, she must have sneaked into the forbidden room, seen the butchered bodies, and understood what he really was underneath all his fine clothes and manners. In my story, though, I changed that a little and made the bloody key bring her help rather than trouble. I changed that on purpose because from what I've seen, curiosity and nosiness and getting things straight usually do work out for the best in the end. Grown-ups changed the story in other places because they thought kids would be too scared if they were told that Bluebeard cut up little boys and not just grown-up women. I disagree. The scariest stories are the ones that have had bits chopped off of them and buried here and there. The grown-ups also took out the part about Saint Joan and the Bishop because they think kids will be bored by all that old-time religion. But I don't think it's boring, any of it. It's just a little mixed up and complicated like most of the rest of life, so I have tried to put it all back together the way it might have really happened, because the scariest thing in the world, maybe the only thing too frightening to bear, is not knowing what really happened, and worrying that perhaps nobody will ever tell you, or let you tell them, exactly all of how it really and truly came to pass.

MISSIONARIES
AND PASTORS

ROBERT SOUTHWELL

AN UNDISCOVERED LETTER FROM
ROBERT SOUTHWELL S.J.

They say best men are molded out of faults,
And for most, become much more the better
For being a little bad.

—WILLIAM SHAKESPEARE, *Measure for Measure*

I trust that we shall, once in heaven,
see each other full merrily.

—SAINT THOMAS MORE, to his executioner

ROBERT SOUTHWELL

SAINT ROBERT SOUTHWELL, Jesuit martyr and poet, was born in Norfolk, England, in 1561 and was hanged, then drawn and quartered at Tyburn, near London, on February 21, 1595. He is commemorated on February 21. He said at his trial that he had been on earth the same number of years as our Lord. His brief life was encompassed by the reign of Queen Elizabeth I, a monarch Southwell much admired. Like Shakespeare, he addressed many of his writings to her.

The Southwell family, despite their nominal Catholicism, retained favor with the Queen, in part because Robert's father and brother were willing to attend Anglican services on ceremonial occasions and did not publicly defy Elizabeth's insistence that the monarch was head of the church. Robert, on the other hand, spent his life defying this principle. He joined the new Jesuit order as a teenager in France. His imagination was caught by the life and death of Edmund Campion, the first English Jesuit martyr, who was, like Southwell, a poet and essayist. Robert Southwell never condemned the Catholics who outwardly conformed with the new official church. He realized how intolerable it was for Catholics to remain Catholics in a land where this was defined as treason. Southwell simply believed that it was worse to try to live a falsehood. The Pope was head of the church, not the Queen, and that was the only truth he could live by.

Throughout the forty-five years of Elizabeth's reign, English Jesuits smuggled themselves to the island from France in disguise to provide the sacraments to Catholics there. Three hundred of these Jesuits were caught and executed. This in no way belies Elizabeth's reputation for religious tolerance. It took her Catholic sister, Mary, only five years to burn three hundred "heretics" at the stake.

The cat-and-mouse pursuits and escapes of these illegal Jesuits, the Queen's anti-Jesuit police (called "poursuivants"), and the great Catholic families who concealed and aided the fugitives provide the highest of sixteenth-century adventures. Topcliffe, the most infamous of the poursuivants, plays the villain in most of these escapades. A few of Southwell's narrow escapes are recorded in his letters to his superiors. One of the narrowest occurred when the poursuivants entered the mansion of the Vaux family while Southwell was serving Mass on the upper floor. The lady of the house rushed to the hall and obstructively feigned a swoon in the middle of the only staircase. Her nine-year-old daughter dashed up to fan her, further blocking the staircase as she explained that the intruders had better put away their swords since her mother always fainted at the sight of arms and would faint again as soon as she awoke unless all swords had been put out of sight. While the poursuivants were being outfaced by this nine-year-old, Southwell had time to conceal all traces of the Mass and himself in a "priest-hole" constructed inside the walls of the chapel. Most of these hiding places were made by a lay Jesuit carpenter named Nicholas Owen who died under torture rather than reveal the locations of the countless priest-holes he had built. Blessed Nicholas Owen is remembered on March 12.

Southwell was sheltered by other powerful Catholic families, most notably by the Arundels. Lord Arundel was confined in the tower at the same time as Southwell. The two were never allowed to meet, but Arundel's little dog did occasionally trot into Southwell's cell. One of the things that endeared Southwell to his jailer was the solemn way he blessed this little dog before sending it back to its master.

The Bellamys were the third great family associated with Southwell, as you will learn in the following letter, which tells some stories of his later adventures and has much to say about the Bellamys.

AN UNDISCOVERED LETTER FROM ROBERT SOUTHWELL, S.J.

TOWER OF LONDON
CHRISTMAS, 1594

To: Father Henry Garnett and through him to General Aquaviva and other superiors and comrades in the Society of Jesus

You must know how closely I have been guarded these two years and more since Topcliffe seized me and took me to his own house to torture. I have since been kept prisoner in the tower except for three months in the dungeons. It was my father, I think, who through official protest got me out of the dungeons. Still they keep me away from all visitors because the Queen and her henchmen are afraid the public will learn of my sufferings, which, knowing London, I am certain many already have done, despite all precautions.

These many months I have thought and sorted through my memories and schemed to find some stratagem to guide a letter to you as has been my habit and happy duty. This need is made more urgent now by the circumstances of my imprisonment. In the past, we have found clever ruses. You will remember the time I baked a letter into a loaf of bread. We packed it into a basket of three dozen and sent them across the Channel, where they made a brave feast for our boys in the Jesuit school at Saint Omers. I am told the oilskin wasn't found until the last loaf was being eaten. I have heard that Father Gerard, when he disguises himself as a soldier (which is in fact no disguise but rather his own true self emerging), rolls letters up inside the barrel of his musket. I recollect the recipe for invisible ink and also that cipher that makes it seem cabbages are being counted rather than Catholic souls. None of those devices avails here as I am not allowed paper, quill, or even the visitors who could smuggle such things in and out.

They allowed my sister to come one time only. She brought fresh shirts and my breviary (which you must have found, Henry, in that last hiding place). There were two of Topcliffe's men, though, watching us every moment so I dared nothing knowing that Topcliffe aches for any excuse to torture or imprison her as a way to hurt me.

Now you will ask, in that case, whence comes this letter? I shall answer although I know how distasteful you will find my reply. For one thing, you will say I've gone as mad as some of the best of us have done in the confines of priest-holes and dungeons. (You will remember that day of our annual retreat in 1591 when Baddesley Clinton was raided by Topcliffe and his poursuivants. There we were, ten or more Jesuit priests standing up to our necks in sewage, in that cunning hole Owen had constructed, stuck there for twelve hours while they searched for us. Then old Father Stanney started raving and after a time began bashing any of us that moved and I made things worse by trying not to laugh.) Well, I'm not gone mad, but I am having visions again, which I know you hate. When I see that face you make at the merest threat of a vision I'm clearly reminded of the mathematician you once were, who still lives at the heart of you. Remember when I came home from that December visit to the North and told you how I had seen the Christ Child floating in light in the forest? You said it would make a good poem, and it did make a fine one which I was singing earlier today to keep Christmas morning:

As I in hoary winter's night stood shivering in the snow,
Surprised I was with sudden heat which made my heart to glow;

Robert Southwell

159

And lifting up a fearful eye to view what fire was near,

A pretty babe all shining bright did in the air appear.

Looking back, though, I understand that you wanted it made into a poem so as to take it out of reality because when a vision is cluttering your reality you begin to feel miserable. This has been hard for me to comprehend because it is the opposite for me. It is when I cannot yet see the vision that reality becomes oppressive, eerie, and foreign-seeming. It is the ordinary, simple, cozy reality of that Burning Babe, though, that fills my memory still, and that I never did quite get poured out of me and into my poem. At the moment of seeing the Babe, an absolute certainty swept over me, a certainty too solid to put into words. He was mine and I was His and there was nothing else. Nothing else.

All the rest of the day I walked through a world of clarity and certitude, a world I had never before inhabited. I walked on until I came that evening to a fine country manor that turned out to be the home of the local sheriff, which is always the best place to lodge if you are an outlaw and a fugitive. They were keeping their English Christmas that night with ale and greens and the yule log and gypsy dancers and masquers—I remember one dressed as a bear and one as a horse. We had kept Christmas in the same way all through my childlhood but it was as if I were seeing it all for the first time. On that clear night I first came to understand how deeply pagan this whole land remains after all these centuries of missionaries. This is why the Christ Child stays outside in the forest burning to be let in. Knowing that thing, sad as it was to know, was the mind's own pure joy, a grace that seemed to run direct from God. At once I could see the sense and the profit in all those ruined priories that litter this England, even old Saint Faith's where I used to play as a child. They are God's outward sign that the Church has never touched this people. I understood, too, why God had kept telling me, each time I asked him to allow me to be sent as a missionary to the pagans, to go to England. He was only trying to be agreeable, and I mistook it for argument. "How endless is your labyrinth of bliss, where to be lost the sweetest finding is."

The vision this time is different. I choose to think of it as an angel, although I suppose it could be a demon, or a hallucination, or even a misplaced wood sprite. What I see is a man, absolutely perfect in every way, who steps through a place in the wall as if it were a door. At first I didn't know what to do with him, so I talked to him and told him my worries. Then one day he came with a quill pen and a scrivener's box (with such priceless milky white parchment) as if he had just picked up the entire kit from a scribe at Saint Paul's. He takes dictation wonderfully. There is something enormous in his capacity to listen which fills me with hope and joy and makes the writing better, I pray. I have already given him some poems I had made in my mind and was afraid my vagrant memory might allow to drift away. My thinking gets a bit rusty here with no one to talk to. For some reason, though, this solitary confinement does not incline me to loneliness. The masses I celebrate, the poems I write, the personalities I try to understand—all within the confines of my own imagination—seem far more intense and full of life than any of those things had ever felt in reality.

Perhaps it is the influence of the angel. I wonder sometimes where he takes the things he writes for me. Sometimes I imagine that there is a secret printing press in heaven and that this angel is carrying my baggage on to that place before me. When I arrive, I imagine that Campion and all the other good Jesuits who have needed a well-hidden press will be there and we will fill the heavenly library with radical pamphlets and read each other's brave words most merrily. This letter, too, may be headed for that same press. If the letter does reach you, I must confess a wish that you may think impolite. Please do not reply. It would unbalance things here if you did. One part of not being lonely is that in my mind flows a round always sung between my life and my death. They make a kind of music which it pains me to interrupt. I never dreamed my death was so old in me or so wise. The voices complete one another's sentences. I wish only to listen here forever. One of my early poems began to describe this, but the reality goes on beyond.

> I live, but such a life as never dies;
>
> I die, but such a death as never ends.
>
> My death to end, my dying life denies,
>
> And life my giving death no whit amends.

Now I come to a matter which I hope does reach you, although I suppose if these pages merely reach God, He will know how to proceed. I have been anxious lest Anne Bellamy be blamed in any way for my arrest. She is at the center of it, of course, but the scheming and active evil is Topcliffe's alone. One could say that his principal pleasure lies in capturing and torturing priests. One could also say that he does what he does for the money, and for the money alone. He receives from the Queen a bounty for each one of us captured and he gleans other monies as well, such as payment from Catholics for visits to and information about prisoners, the goods he confiscates from priests and other Catholics captured, and bribes from the wealthy who may wish a Catholic enemy removed. Topcliffe specializes in manufacturing evidence, which is always accepted in this unfortunate system as genuine so long as the defendant is Catholic.

As you can see, the man fascinates me and I have spent many days pondering the qualities of his soul. He is immune to reason. The idea of honor has no place in his cosmos, yet he is the most self-righteous fellow I have ever met. Even though a child could prove with sums that he does this evil work for the pounds, shillings, and pence it gets him, his own conception would be otherwise. He would say he is leading a crusade to rid the kingdom of its enemies and he is able to feel more moral in saying that than I have felt ever in my life. His morality consists in a belief that he deserves all goods and honors that exist in the world and that the only reason he has not gotten them yet is that others have stolen them from him. For him to deprive anyone of any gift of God whatsoever, including life itself, is simple justice according to these lights. I pray day and night for the Queen who employs him. How can she not see that the craven conscience which justifies killing me could as easily be turned to the justification of her own excecution? He began boasting one day of his sexual conquest of the Queen and I, from my chains, challenged him to a duel. He apologized. I believe he was cunning enough to fear that I might someday repeat those words of his to the grave hazard of his head.

To know Topcliffe in a nutshell is to know his invention which he calls "Topcliffe's rack," which in fact has affinities with the torture of the pulleys as well as with the Roman rack. It is quickest described as a kind of crucifixion. One's hands are chained spread-eagled to the wall at such a height that one's feet cannot reach the floor. The body's own weight racks and stretches and shreds the muscles. It is typical of Topcliffe that he loves this device so because it leaves no marks and thus can cause no scandal.

He carries a special hatred for me because he believes me to possess a certain grace of speech and bearing which most certainly must have been plundered in its entirety from him at the very beginning of the aforementioned conspiracy against him. He is the only human being I have known that I would call ugly. This has nothing to do with the way God made him, but with the anger and hatred that inhabit his every movement, his every sentence, the very bones of his face. I told him once from the rack when he was cursing the fair look in my face that God could make him beautiful if he would just give God room to work on him. That was the time he left me there to die and I would have done except that Nicholas Jones cut me down.

Nicholas is Anne Bellamy's husband now, so I am back to

that tale of tragedy. Topcliffe had Anne arrested in January, six months before he captured me. Topcliffe arrested her, tortured her, raped her, and broke her body and her soul for no other reason than to form her into a tool and a trap for capturing me; so the truth is that I am the cause of her suffering rather than she the cause of mine. She has always been one of those people with whom I have been waiting patiently to meet the rest of who they are. At first one assumes that she is simply young or shy or quiet, but then one keeps waiting and waiting and waiting and there is never any more of her to meet. Of course now, after Topcliffe, she is no more than a shell. I wonder where the soul goes in such cases? It must be compressed down somehow to the size of a thimble or smaller and then hidden so carefully that even the owner in time forgets where it was put for safekeeping. When I first met her, the family had still not recovered from the Babington affair.

As I have written before, Father Babington never had any intention of killing Queen Elizabeth and placing Mary, Queen of Scots, on the throne. No priest would do that. It is adventure enough just to give the sacraments, without hazarding anything more. These lies and forgeries were put around by Topcliffe, but once the hunt was on it was to the Bellamy house that Babington fled, and they were brave enough to take him in. Poor Babington was almost done for by then anyway, having lived in the forest for weeks in the dead of winter. You know how it all ended: Babington and two Bellamy brothers were arrested; one brother "killed himself" in prison (so they say); the others were executed. Anne was faced with living out a counterfeit of her former life, going through all the forms of belonging to a great family but with no invitations, no suitors. Even the Catholic families shunned them because they believed Topcliffe's lie that the priest Babington had committed real treason rather than the simple and normal treason that being a Catholic priest has become. So in a way there was not that much left to break in Anne by the time Topcliffe got hold of her. With his techniques, though, he would have broken a much stronger woman. After three months she was cold, filthy with lice, pregnant from his rapes, and terrified of death.

That was when the assistant, Nicholas Jones, entered the play to show her the way to make everything right. Nicholas seems really to believe those things that Topcliffe merely pretends as motives. Whenever he has a spare moment, you will find him reading his Wycliffe Bible. He has forsaken dancing, drink, music, and games and seems convinced that this insures him against all other sin for the balance of his life. His father was a crofter on the Bellamy estates and Nicholas seems certain that Jehovah has determined that he should possess certain farms there that he has coveted since childhood. These were the farms Anne asked as her dowry. I cannot teach myself to dislike Nicholas entirely, perhaps because he has saved my life as well as Anne's. However, Jones is Topcliffe's creature body and perhaps soul. I remember an afternoon when Topcliffe stood laughing at a prisoner hanging in chains and begging to be let down. Anne turned to Topcliffe with a look that held the beginnings of a forgotten revulsion, and Nicholas, seeing the look, hit her so hard in the face tht she fell to the floor.

What I want you to understand clearly is that Anne Bellamy cannot be held accountable for my capture. I did not know all these things when I got her note that June night. I knew some of it. I reasoned she might need confession, or a blessing on her irregular marriage, or that she might be summoning me into a trap. I went to her. Even though I know now that she called me into an ambush, if she sent me the same message today, I would go to her. I sometimes wrestle with the bleak image of a time that may come when every Catholic in this unfortunate country will have been destroyed as Anne Bellamy has been.

For myself, what prison has done to me is the precise opposite of destruction. It has mended me into a wholeness I never believed could be mine. Of course my body is broken, but somehow that does not signify much. I fight the pain. Any

Robert Southwell

165

movement—walking, even talking—brings pressure against the ruptured muscles. This is sudden agony. Pray for me that I might bear this during the hours of standing and defending myself at the trial, and at the end when I ride to Tyburn and speak my last words at the scaffold. Also there is much anger to bear and contain. I have thought that perhaps Topcliffe racked me so many times—ten times he hanged me up on his rack—because he noticed that throughout the first four times, I was so angry thinking about Anne and the way she had been so used and deliberately broken, that in some sense I was not properly attending to the pain.

Please pray God also to forgive me my unfailing politeness to Topcliffe which has been an enormous comfort to my soul, but which enrages Topcliffe and thus provides, I fear, further occasion for him to sin. So this life is not without troubles: "Unmeddled joys here to no man befall, who least hath some who most hath never all." Nevertheless "joy" is the word I must use to describe all this, and at times I wonder if that is entirely normal or fitting in me. I keep thinking that a proper martyr, a Campion, for example, would feel differently, would accept the fact as a necessary evil but with sadness and regret and the awful dread that tormented Christ in Gethsemane. Pray for me that this difference in me be but difference, not sin. This joy I feel is gratitude as well, a simple relief that God has found this place for me where at last I belong. I can explain this best with a story.

One day while Topcliffe was racking me he was torturing also another man, a young gypsy who was hanging in his chains a few paces down the wall from me. Topcliffe, as it turns out, is a hunter of gypsies, as well as a hunter of Jesuits, and for many of the same reasons. He hates them with a self-righteous fervor, and the landowners bribe him to get rid of gypsy camps on their property. Now most of you have heard the tale of how, when I was a babe, an old gypsy woman stole me away, substituting her own son for me in my crib, and how it was only because my own dear nurse came in immediately and noticed the difference that the gypsy was caught in the courtyard and I was reclaimed. What I have never told anyone is that I have always worried that maybe they got me mixed in the end after all and the real Robert Southwell has been tinkering and dancing to the moon all these years, while I have been playing merely at pretending to be me. That day in the rack, watching the gypsy suffer as I suffered, I saw there was no reason to feel separated inside myself. There has been one path, and one only, for me from the beginning of eternity. I have earned the rack and the gibbet as honorably as a Southwell and a gentleman and a Jesuit as ever I would have done as a gypsy minstrel. The mystery of who I am dissolved that day. "God's gift am I, and none but God shall have me."

It is all paradox here. In solitary confinement, I am less lonely and more free than ever before. It was in the chains of the rack that I first felt comfort and solace. In the very death-grip of my enemies, I find myself surrounded by kindness. The lieutenant jailer here refers to me as "that saint" in a tone so filled with irony and fond regret that a friend could fall into such error that he puts me into my place at once. He is fond of court gossip. Some evenings when he serves me my bread and water, we both let our imaginations run free. I tell him tales of the grand houses on the Strand, of the Vaux family and the Arundels. We talk of poets, Jonson's drinking bouts, Marlowe's duels, Shakespeare's passionless passions.

"Shakespeare's the only one of us who will die in his bed," I say, and then I can see through my tears that I am enjoying the play better than my audience. Thank God and you, my brothers, for giving me these seven years to be in England and be Catholic.

YOURS IN CHRIST,
ROBERT SOUTHWELL, S.J.

Robert Southwell

POSTSCRIPT

Robert Southwell was tried and hanged in February 1595. Mrs. Anne Jones was the only witness against him at the trial. He said not a word against Anne's testimony, but spoke eloquently against Topcliffe and his torture devices. One of Elizabeth's advisers wrote, "No wonder they trust these Jesuits with their lives." Topcliffe behaved so badly at the trial that many said this precipitated his fall from royal favor and his own prosecution for bribery. Elizabeth's favorite at court, Lord Mountjoy, spoke with Southwell in Newgate Prison on the eve of the execution, and the next day, when Topcliffe tried to begin the drawing and quartering before Southwell was properly dead, it was Mountjoy himself who pushed Topcliffe aside, and pulled down on the legs of the hanging man to hasten death. Mountjoy said, "I cannot answer for the man's religion, but God grant that my soul may be with his."

After the execution, Garnett scoured Southwell's possessions for some sort of message or sign about his last days, but no letter was ever found. The only trace that Garnett could discover was, on one page of Southwell's breviary, picked out finely with a pin, the name Jesus. He counted and recounted the pinpricks in each letter. He ran his fingers over the page again and again. When the young priests asked what he was doing, he smiled his thin, hard smile and said he was reading the last undiscovered letters of Robert Southwell.

JUNIPERO SERRA

IN PAYMENT FOR THE CHICKENS

Yet it was surely impossible that we should halt
on the edge of this world of mystery when our very souls
were tingling with impatience to push forward and
to pluck the heart from it.

—SIR ARTHUR CONAN DOYLE, *The Lost World*

JUNIPERO SERRA

JUNIPERO SERRA, THE FRANCISCAN who came to the New World in 1749 and left it, for death, in 1784 is not yet a saint, not yet even beatified. Venerable is as far as he's gotten up the saint ladder. That came in 1985 amid street demonstrations pro and contra, mostly contra. Two hundred years after his death he arouses such passion still, and that is what smells most to me of sanctity.

Native American activists have been quick to point out that the most palpable and quantifiable result of Junípero's missionizing was the near or total extinction of every tribe he tried to touch. One must remember, though, that almost all of the "noble savages" "discovered" by Europeans in the Age of Exploration died regardless of how greatly they were admired or respected. I think of Pocahontas, received as a princess in London, feted by the queen, then sickening there and dying at age twenty-two. Native Americans reacted to Europeans as if they were a disease, and they were that to them, not only because of the viruses nourished during centuries of separation, but even more because of the ideas that had incubated.

In this context Junípero had somewhat the reputation of an antibiotic. Those American Indians who had recently turned up at one of his sermons were said to have a survival edge against the deadly epidemics. Still, these recent demonstrators remind us that Franciscans in the New World, were not like Franciscans in the Old World greeting Brother Sun penniless and barefoot in infinite trust. In the New World, Franciscans often took charge of the Inquisition, burning and destroying American Indian holy places and art. Some Franciscans became toadies and apologists for their military coexplorers, bending their missions to economic exploitation and political subjugation of the natives. If there were any clerical good guys in the New World, they were Jesuits, even Dominicans, but when you look at it cold and hard, the likeliest reconstruction is that none of them were good guys. Europeans all carried with them the germs of Western civilization, that deadliest of all diseases. Yes, the Devil's advocate has plenty of ammunition in Junípero's case.

Somehow, though, I find myself ranged on Junípero's side. My partisanship is not logical, not even quite coherent. Part of it is that I like Franciscans. In some ways they make good inquisitors. They're not impressed or intimidated by the majesty of mere things. A radical Franciscan would have no more qualms about destroying a Kwakiutl mask than about destroying a pretentious cathedral like the one built to house Francis's tiny Portiuncula church. Francis zapped that cathedral with an earthquake in the early part of the present century. The Portiuncula remained standing, untouched there in the center of the shambles. However, nobody got the message that time either. They built another huge, ugly marble cathedral right back up again. There's no telling what Francis will have to do to get rid of this one. (Junípero's basilica met a similar fate in the Great San Francisco Earthquake of 1906, which his old adobe mission next door weathered handily.)

I'm on Junípero's side, too, because of the terrible and amazing midst-of-the-wilderness place that is America. I think of the tiny island world of Majorca, Junípero's home, cultivated like a walled garden. Then I think of Junípero walking from Mexico City to Northern California, in a kind of intermittent delirium in which all men on horseback became Saint Martin, all ferrymen angels, and every family who gave him shelter and food the Holy Family. I think of my kinfolks and ancestors who were trying to get a grip on the vastness of America at about the same time, on the other edge of the continent. Their stories are about as unpretty as Junípero's stories.

What I am trying to say is that I believe I know what Junípero was up against. There is this terrible beautiful vastness to America, which becomes a kind of cruelty. It keeps coming out at us from this American earth still—even though we've paved most of it over trying to bury it or at least hold it down under layers and layers of concrete.

I think of the Franciscans in Arizona who thought they had their Indians fully missionized until someone told them about the cave where the weather lives. Off went the Franciscans, holy water and unenthusiastic Indians in tow to exorcise these demons. They rolled the stone away from the door of the cave. Suddenly thunder boomed, lightning crackled, rain poured down, and the wind blew like a hurricane. The Franciscans rolled the stone back into place, and if all of us were as wise as they, that stone would still be there.

I think of a story the Acoma tell about the first Franciscan who came there. Acoma Pueblo was inaccessible because it stood on a mesa scalable only by one carefully guarded path. That's why the Acoma had chosen to live there. They didn't like strangers, especially conquistador-type strangers. The Acoma took arms against the first such party who came to their country and they lost the battle. In retaliation for the trouble they'd given, the Spaniards hacked off the right foot of every warrior. One wonders how many generations are required for the decontamination of such an action. More than have yet tolled at Acoma Pueblo.

Nonetheless, long ago and within living memory of the atrocity there came this Franciscan who ignored the unscalability of the mesa, ignored the implacable hatred from the Acoma who watched from above, hoping for the pleasure of seeing him fall, perhaps even of pushing him if he got far enough. As the Franciscan climbed barefoot, rock to rock, the Acoma headman's little daughter leaned out too far and fell, miraculously not to her death but to a level patch right in front of the Franciscan, who scooped her up in one arm and kept on climbing. This was a Franciscan the Acoma decided they could endure. Alas, though, nothing lasts forever.

The next Franciscan was less good and the next even worse and at last the Acoma found themselves under the heel of a Franciscan who was a compulsive gardener. Not a major vice, you may think, but bear in mind there is no water on the Acoma mesa. No water and no topsoil. The Acoma carried every basket of earth, every jug of water, as the garden became larger and larger. The Franciscan never even realized the Indians minded the work, until one day, as he sat in his room in the chapel (the bricks of course had been hand-carried up the trail) several large Acoma men came in, picked up the Franciscan and threw him off the mesa. (Willa Cather tells this last part of the story in *Death Comes to the Archbishop*, and some Junípero stories as well.)

Not that all the gardens were so hard on the Indians. The reconstructions of Junípero's walled mission gardens have an orderliness and yet a profusion and variety, as if in each one he had recreated his tiny home island. Near Santa Fe there is a massive apricot tree planted, so they say, by the early Franciscans before they were all killed in the Pueblo revolt. There is such peace in that knotted, manybranched weathered old tree, that still-living witness to a quaint and wondrous dream that all New Mexico somehow could be transformed into a vast, well-ordered orchard.

They say that years after Junípero died, years after the missions fell into ruins, years after Western diseases and diseased Westernness had killed all but lonely remnants of Junípero's tribes, American Indians used to come to his ruined gardens on holy days and play fragments of Gregorian chants on homemade violins.

Perhaps that is enough. We'll see what the Devil's Advocate has to say in reply.

IN PAYMENT FOR
THE CHICKENS

F ather Junípero Serra was one of those people who can only learn in the grip of a blinding rage. Recognizing that about himself was one of the blessings that had softened his old age. The flogging helped, too, and the walking. This present walk was a short one, two days only, and he had had to bring the old woman and the boy to carry the chickens. None of the men would come with him anymore. They said that with Father Junípero you never knew where you might end. Maybe at San Francisco, maybe in the heavens, perhaps at Mexico City, or, more likely, in the inferno. Why did even the old woman come? For love of God? For love of Junípero? Back home the parish priests said there was always one hovering crone smitten with the local parson. Thank goodness that among these pagans the women, at least, wore clothing. The men roamed as naked as Adam.

The boy, Bendito, was very proud that he had been allowed to carry the chickens. It was, of course, he, not his mother, who was in love with the crazy old priest. His mother merely let the boy love in peace. Bendito had never seen plain longing in the old man's eyes, except when old Junípero talked of the chickens or of the bells. The bells Bendito could understand, but these chickens were smaller than he had thought, and more fat and ill-tempered, and they made incessant, nerve-wrenching noises. The old man always talked of food for the children when he spoke of chickens, so perhaps their magic was in the eating, like the magic of the eating in the Mass.

That night, on the road, Junípero dreamed about the chickens. He dreamed he was following the dark red rooster through a small door into the chicken house. Looking up, he saw how beautifully the nest above was constructed. A hen sat brooding on the nest and her trilling filled Junípero with rapture beyond all telling. Through the weave of her nest, Junípero could see the nine perfectly formed eggs that she was warming. White they were, like mission churches, and he imaged that if only he could get a bit closer he would see the shadows of the towers through the shells. The dream ended so suddenly that he awoke simply from the pain of losing it.

Junípero awoke to see the empty cage in the moonlight, and the chicken bones in the fire, and the twisted-off heads of the rooster and of both hens. The old woman and the boy were still snoring, cradling their bloated bellies.

The rage of disappointment and frustration drove Junípero first into the cage. After he had battered that thing into sharp splinters, the flogging began. For several hours, the old man flogged himself with what was left of the now futile chicken coop. In these rages, Junípero had no choice. He could flog himself, or give in to the need to tear into that greedy old woman and that thoughtless boy.

Toward the end, Bendito, now awake and watching, began to gag, because the broken sticks seemed to find no more flesh in the old priest, only blood. Hour after hour, Bendito watched Junípero tearing into his own flesh. Hours, also, it had taken for the eating of the chickens. That eating had gone past hunger, past taste, until Bendito felt only a numb reaching-out for the magic: the eating magic, that had not, after all, been the true or proper magic inside the chickens.

It was just before dawn that Junípero opened his eyes and, through the sweat and pain, found them focused on the cock's head at his feet. It opened its beak and it crowed three times, and Junípero fell to his knees and tried to think. Perhaps he was not seeing the thing correctly, thought Junípero, even now, even with the flogging. That had been Peter's problem, too, when the cock crowed for him. Peter had not yet seen the situation correctly. He had, in fact, got everything entirely backwards.

Later that year, when Advent came, Junípero told Bendito that the boy could play Balthazar, the third wise man, in the crèche on Christmas Day. Bendito said he was too young for such an honor. The old priest said, please, he still owed the boy for the chickens.

Bendito felt that he alone deserved the honor of paying for the chickens. Also, he did not feel like a wise man. He felt like a devil. So he asked the other priest to tell him the devil stories and to draw the devil pictures in the sand. Bendito made a triangular wooden mask with horns, stained red. He made the Devil's tail out of rope and wound a larger green-dyed rope around himself to be the Devil's snake.

It was in this guise that Bendito came to the Christ Child that Christmas, bringing, not myrrh, but two carvings he had made. The first was a wooden rooster full of anger, in red and black, and the other was a carved hen, painted white, whose neck curved in just the way to make your heart ache.

Junípero was playing Joseph that Christmas, and he took the chickens in his hands and said that the baby could not keep them just yet. The Family were about to flee into Egypt and Herod's soldiers might hear the clucking of the chickens and find the Child to kill him. Joseph asked if someone might keep the chickens until the Child grew older. José, an older man with grown children, came forward and said that he would guard the animals.

And so it went. The next Christmas it was José who came in the mask of the Devil and another family who agreed to keep the chickens until the Child grew older. They began to talk about the magic in the cock and to keep him hooded, except on feast days. Too many foolish and envious visitors became ill after looking into the rooster's bright and terrible eyes. Everyone said that the mother hen would sing you to heavenly sleep each night, but that, marvelous and comforting as she was, if you kept her one hour beyond your one year's trust, the cock would destroy you and your family entirely.

Christmasses passed. Floggings passed, and walks. As Junípero grew older, he often forgot which mission it was that he was walking to, and began to imagine he was walking toward heaven. All the thirst and hunger and weakness and pain would disappear as he imagined how, with the next stumble, he would fall, not into earth, but into whatever that other was.

This day, God had given Junípero so many chances to fall, that the old man was sure that the next one would be that lucky one through the magic door. So it was with some resentment that he noticed the pleasant house beneath the cottonwoods just ahead. A man and a woman came out to carry him inside. The woman had to lift the spoon for the old priest to get some soup into him. There was a child of three or four playing near the fire and there was the calming sound of brooding hens. Junípero was asleep before he could ask where the hens had come from or whether he might have one or two of the chicks when they hatched.

The next morning the family were out. Plowing, thought Junípero. He had slept late. He had his bearings now. It was a half day's walk to Carmel. He would come back tomorrow and say thank you.

Junípero told the story of these new neighbors by the by as part of the larger telling of the journey. But Bendito saw the miracle in it as soon as the old man mentioned about the chickens. He crossed himself. "The chickens came from us, my father. They are the ones I ate. Herod's soldiers have gone now; so Saint Joseph lets the Child have his chickens. They are the ones that we have been guarding for Him until He was older."

Father Junípero went out the next day, nonetheless. They found the cottonwoods, but there was no house there, and no family. Bendito put up a cross, but Junípero said it must have been a different stand of cottonwoods, and kept on looking. Junípero still had hopes of bargaining for a few of the chicks once the eggs hatched.

It was only because Junípero had failed so utterly and so repeatedly at introducing chickens to Carmel Mission that he understood when, on the twelfth day of his illness, he awoke to the soothing clucking of brooding hens and the intermittent sunbursts of cockcrows, that this was his death. He glanced quickly around to make sure he had given everything away. Then he felt with dismay the scratch of the blanket over his body. He had already torn it in half and given the first to an old woman. Why ever had he kept this other awkward half lingering here to embarrass him?

"Bendito!" he cried.

His friend moved closer.

"Take the blanket, my friend. For the love of my soul, take the blanket, please, in payment for the chickens…"

Bendito was still holding the blanket and trying to explain how, in his view, no further payment was needed, when he noticed that the battered old man had died.

POSTSCRIPT

Junípero Serra died August 28, 1784 at the Carmel Mission, at about the same time English-speaking usurpers on the East Coast were adopting a constitution from which they excluded their slaves. You can still visit the room where he died at Carmel, and you can also visit the other California missions he founded. I particularly love the ruins at San Juan Capistrano and the sudden silence of the urban missions in San Francisco and San Diego with their four-foot-thick adobe walls.

I have told you a story about the wild mystical Junípero, but there are stories, equally compelling, about Junípero the polished professor of theology and Junípero the wily administrator, perennial thorn in the side of every military commander assigned to him. It was this latter Junípero who negotiated with the viceroy in advance a pardon for any pagan who might kill him. Pagans by their very nature kill missionaries, he argued, just as missionaries have it in their natures to get themselves killed. If anyone were to be punished in such an event it should be the military guards assigned to protect him. They would be the only players obviously and by definition to have failed.

Still, seen as a man of his time, Junípero begins to recede from us. It is when he is closest to his beloved Indian converts that he comes closest to us as well. "In fact all the pagans have pleased me," he wrote, "but these in particular have stolen my heart." They stole from each other always, Junípero and his charges, because each side knew the utter value of the other. Early on, the natives tried to steal Junípero's glasses. From his dead body they took locks of hair and scraps of his habit while the good Franciscans patiently explained that these things had no merit, that there had been no canonization. Those Indians knew better. Like Junípero, counting and recounting the 6,736 souls he had baptized, they knew ultimate value when they saw it.

Theirs was a doomed and tragic love full of funny moments because no one spoke the same language. When Junípero planted a cross, the Indians tried to answer in kind, surrounding this first odd gift with feathers and broken arrows and fresh sardines. Later, when the natives attacked a mission, groping for some way to express the unspeakable frustration of their impossible situation, the Franciscan padre came out to them all alone and playing a barrel organ. The rebels listened to that music, and then, satisfied that for the moment they had been heard and understood, they melted away into the wilderness.

JEAN VIANNEY

PARISH PRIEST
AND SOMETIME DESERTER FROM
NAPOLEON'S GRAND ARMY

There is but one way…to give oneself to God—
that is, to give oneself entirely and to keep nothing for oneself.
The little that one keeps is only good to trouble one
and make one suffer.

—Jean Vianney

JEAN VIANNEY

JEAN VIANNEY ("Jean" is pronounced like "John" but with a soft "z" thrown in at the beginning) was part of that century-long identity crisis following the French Revolution when France made itself and imagined itself into what we think of still as France.

Artists, musicians, and writers like Degas, Offenbach, and Dumas *fils* gave us a dream Paris filled with dancing, beautiful women, champagne, hectic gaiety, and romance. It was this Paris young soldiers sang songs and told stories about through world wars that seem now, despite their documented destructiveness, somehow so much less real than the Paris dreams which helped lure men to die there. I still recall that day in college when the professor was trying to convey some nuance of meaning in a story by Unamuno. "Someday," he said, "you, too, will stand on a bridge overlooking the Seine beside someone you love, and then you will know."

Actually I had already been to France as a child, in a way. Not only to France but to nineteenth-century France somewhere in the neighborhood of Arles. When I was eight, an old wartime comrade of my dad's turned up one spring at our ranch in Texas, intent on painting our wheat fields. When the prairie winds blew his canvas off the easel, he muttered that the same thing had happened to Van Gogh, and rambled on about that previous incarnation. He had been through landing after landing in the South Pacific and watched friends die and had lost some part of himself there, maybe his mind. Later that summer he turned to painting my portrait. It hangs still on the wall of my parents' dining room, a grave blond child in a blue shirt. Forty years later I met its twin staring back at me from a museum wall in Amsterdam. The catalogue said it was the postmaster's son, age seven, painted by Van Gogh at Arles right after he painted his wheat fields. I would be curious to know what the nineteenth-century postmaster's son thought he knew about Texas.

While Van Gogh was busy painting, Victor Hugo, Dumas *pere*, and others were busy rewriting French history. They started with the recent unintelligibly violent revolution—which was badly in need of a rewrite—and went backward to make all the rest orderly and hero-ic, giving us an imaginary France forever peopled by noble muske-teers, shrewd priests, fetching ladies in distress, young men full of chivalry and idealism, and starving artists.

Amidst all these renovated images, France's modern saints moved to oddly old-fashioned rhythms as if they were pausing in a minuet while everyone else was whirling to the strains of a Strauss waltz. Take Bernadette, whose story you can read in Franz Werfel's *Song of Bernadette*. She did what saintly maids have always done: she saw the Virgin Mary, spoke with Her, did Her bidding. Werfel's book describes the embarrassment felt by Bernadette's contemporaries. How could such a simple story expect an audience in this modern France which had made itself so cosmopolitan, so avant garde, so sophisticated? This France that now set the tone and style for every-thing from clothes to diplomacy? Bernadette was an embarrassment, an anachronism, and, as you will see, so was Jean Vianney. The won-derful and terrible thing about Vianney is that he knew it. He felt the embarrassment even more exquisitely than did his detractors. When they sent around a petition demanding Vianney's dismissal as Curé of Ars, Vianney himself was one of the first to sign.

PARISH PRIEST
AND SOMETIME DESERTER FROM
NAPOLEON'S GRAND ARMY

It hadn't been a good night. The demon in the chimney had stayed awake moaning the whole night through. The demon did not speak human, so its moaning was only a rumbling noise, like a caisson passing or sometimes like a million little rats hopping up and down. Now that the demon had finally quieted down, it was too late for the Father to drop off, too, so he struggled upwards out of the half-sleep in which he had been tossed and turned, perhaps by the demon, he thought, for the bed had moved again from its usual place against the wall to the center of the room, where it stood at a rather jaunty angle.

Father Jean had taught himself to wake up each morning with the same prayer: "Dear God, let the courtyard be empty. Let the entire village of Ars be empty of pilgrims, tourists, cripples, and the overly devout." It was one of the many trials of his faith that each morning after submitting this prayer he lifted the corner of the curtain to a sea of pilgrims standing in the courtyard (this morning in the mud and pouring rain), waiting for Father Jean to come out and start up the magic and mind-reading act which had become the greatest pilgrim sideshow in France. Each morning he counted them and each morning he ran out of fingers and toes. For a long time he had tried adjusting his wake-up hour, hoping to find a time when all the pilgrims would be asleep. These days he was waking up at three o'clock in the morning, but, even at this hour, the vigilant pilgrims were still out there.

Father Jean was not certain what it was that God was trying to do to him, but whatever it was, God was not skipping any days. Not even today, which was Christmas. In the revolution, too, no holidays had been allowed. You might think that Father Jean, who had survived that harrowing, would have gotten used to it by now. But somehow God was even tougher than Robespierre, more implacable, and Jean had hopes for Christmas. Hope always made these moments worse.

Twenty-six pilgrims he counted, plus Philippe with his crutch coming to relieve the boy sleeping by the fire in the kitchen, the boy who had guarded him through the night shift. The mayor was out there, too, probably trying to keep an eye on the Father. Father Jean had been under guard for more than a month now, since the third time that he had run away. This last time, in November, the schoolboys had found him blue and shivering in a cave. Father Jean had refused to come out or answer any of their questions, so the mayor had called in one of the village giants, who lifted up the old priest like a baby and carried him in his arms back home. Father Jean wept bitterly all the way. The mayor had given the schoolmaster and his boys the task of watching the priest. They seemed to understand the Father in some way that the mayor could not. However, since November, the hunted look had not left the Father's eyes, and even some of the boys had begun to be afraid of him.

For the first fifteen years the mayor had been certain that Jean was bad for the town. Jean had closed down all the bars, preached against the country dances, begged without cease for moneys for orphans, widows, the homeless, the sick, and, in fact, for all the lost, futile outcasts extruded of necessity by the decent voting citizenry of Ars. For those fifteen years, the mayor had schemed and plotted to get rid of Father Jean, with some success. (The local bishop had been firmly on the mayor's side from the beginning.) The problem was where to send him. The Father's own wish was to go to a strict, silent order like the Trappists, but his Latin was so terrible, worse even than the mayor's, that the orders had a built-in excuse for not accepting him. The other villages in the diocese had already heard about Father Jean's expensive crusades and the rest (even in the early days there were signs, definite signs, of madness). And all of the other towns were bigger than Ars, and richer, and more influential. This made transfer more than problematic.

Then somehow in the midst of all the mayor's strategies, everything turned upside down, and now the poor mayor seemed doomed to spend an equal span of his life scheming to make the wretched Father *stay* in Ars. Reasoning did not help; the mayor had tried that. "All of us in Ars depend on you for our living and on the pilgrims who come to you, Father. These people buy meals from us, pay for their horses, buy rosaries for you to bless." But the Father's eyes would go blank whenever the mayor tried to explain to him the economics of the situation. Oh well, thought the mayor, turning back toward home and Christmas. The boys would catch him should he try to flee again.

Philippe knocked at the rectory door and hobbled in. The Father was still looking out the window and listening to the demon's snores when he heard the small sob in the back of the boy's mind.

"What's gone wrong?" asked the Father.

"Nothing," said the boy, and demon roared, and Philippe jumped away from the chimney.

"Please do not be afraid," said Father Jean. "It is only the devil." Philippe was trying to edge far away from the chimney, but it was a small room and very empty, because the old priest kept giving away the furniture.

"Nothing," Philippe said again. Jean Vianney was no longer listening to the boy's words but to the thoughts behind them which went something like this: there were endless chilly predawn mornings, stiff and aching knees, good deeds dutifully performed (including these hours of standing guard over the amazing but temperamental mind-reading priest) and a numb unbelievable shock of betrayal. Philippe sat down by the chimney. Once Jean knew everything it was easier for the boy to say it out loud.

"It was supposed to happen today," he said. "I was to wake up today and my leg would be well. I know I had been praying about it correctly. I went over it all again this morning. I have not asked for anything else, only for this, that the leg be well again at Christmas. I prayed it the same way every time, there were no errors. Every day I prayed; every day I was kind and generous to everyone. Still though, this morning, the leg is weak and full of pain just as it has been since that fever last winter."

The Father turned away from the window and tried to look at Philippe. The sounds were terrible, not only the sobs inside the boy's head, but the demon had started muttering in his sleep.

"I'm sorry, Philippe. I thought I'd warned you against praying. Certainly it's a course whose safety I would never recommend, definitely not for children. Let me tell you a story about prayers. When I was a little boy, the soldiers of the French Revolution were everywhere. Soldiers were assigned to find priests or signs pointing to priests. Candles, rosaries, crucifixes—all were suspect. And when a priest was caught, his head was chopped off. We all went to mass in secret, in the dark of night, with the oldest boys standing guard outside. One time a troop of soldiers came marching directly to our door. Looking back I realize there must have been an informer in our group, but in those days I could not yet read the thoughts of others. My brother, who was on guard that night, whistled the alarm, and the priest jumped under my bed. Mother grabbed her pot of rouge, dotted it all over my face, and tucked me in under the covers. By the time the troops knocked at our door, mother was wailing as she let them in. Everyone else took it up, too."

Father Jean was thinking that it had sounded quite a bit like the demon's snores. "Everyone else was kneeling, weeping at my bedside, and I moved around a little, moaning. 'Smallpox,' said my mother, and those sons of the Republic backed out as if someone had just sounded the retreat. Equality, liberty, and justice are good, but they are not much comfort against the smallpox. Now let me tell you the part that made me sad. The priest crawled out from under the bed and finished saying the mass. At the end all of the grown-ups prayed that the terror would end and we would be free to celebrate mass in the open once more. I could not believe that they would pray such a thing. I had thought everyone else was having as much fun that night as I was, fooling those soldiers. I didn't want to go to mass in a mere church, sharing it with people who had never risked their lives for it. The host was my own treasure, too precious to be left without the protection of night, and guards, and camouflage, and secrecy. You see I was praying against them all, but in the end it was their prayers that were heard and answered."

Philippe had been listening intently, "But Father, who could be praying against me in this matter?"

"One can never be certain," said Jean, "but it is quite possible that I myself have been praying against you. Not that I knew it or meant you harm. You know how I dread the tourists. I pray constantly for a stop to all miracles at Ars immediately and forever. The sick pilgrims in particular make me shudder. I would not mind so much if God sent me only criminals and lunatics. I can talk to them. That's why I put the statue of Saint Philomena down at the far end of the church. She doesn't mind the sick ones. Actually it is she you must ask about the leg. Tell her I sent you. She does whatever I ask. But please be discreet about this. After she cures you, just hobble out on your crutch as if it were a normal day, and when you get home, burn the crutch. Whatever you do, don't leave it lying around the church. Such things attract pilgrims the way honey draws flies."

It was time to go. At the door a big fellow wearing the old-fashioned garb of Napoleon's army swung into step with them. He was lame on the same side as Philippe, and their limping strides matched exactly, if Philippe went two for every one of the old man's. The veteran managed his limp with a beautiful cane, intricately carved on every centimeter of its surface.

Father said to him, "You came here to celebrate the anniversary of your wound."

"Twenty-one years ago today. That's when it happened, and it still hurts," said the old soldier. "There's a bullet around the knee somewhere. Every Christmas brings the memory back sharp as the pain. In those days I was still half a child. I still believed that nothing bad could happen to me on Christmas Day. We soldiers were cold and miserable and hungry but even so we were headed home, and I felt safe, even happy. It was Christmas after all. Then a small group of Russian partisans ambushed us. Were you there, Father, on that march? I seem to remember your face."

"People always tell me that they recognize me. I think it's because they see their own memories flickering across my eyes. No, I was not there. I've never been anywhere. I spent my time in the army as a deserter. Not that I ever set out to become a deserter. It was God's gift you might say, like your knee. That first day, I remember, I kept trying to find my unit, but I had a fever and everything kept getting mixed up. I did find them at last but then I fell asleep again and they went on without me. I was very sick and delirious, I think. They could not wake me. When I did wake up I prayed to the Virgin Mary. I put myself into her hands entirely, and she must have been in a whimsical mood because immediately an army captain came along and I told him about my situation and he took me to his encampment in the forest. It was three days before I figured out that he and all his troops were deserters, too, and that I had joined a den of outlaws rather than my regiment. I demanded to be taken to the local authorities. So the captain took me to the mayor in the next village and when he heard my story he took me to his cousin in the country so she could hide me in her barn. By then the Virgin must have had me where she wanted me because I was too sick to move. The sickness went on for days. That was when this thing, this gift of reading thoughts, took hold. It is a kind of scar from that illness.

"When I recovered, I could not understand what had happened to me. I didn't realize I was already hearing other people's thoughts. It's not really exactly like hearing. I don't know how to explain it. It's like remembering, but then you realize that the memory is supposed to be in someone else's mind. For example, I remember it all as clearly as you do, that march through Russia. That moment when you realized it was an attack, when the horses were upon you. When this started, in that barn, I thought I was going mad. Whenever the soldiers came to search, the other deserters and I would crawl inside the haystack. We waited for the searchers to come and push their bayonets into the hay to spear any deserters, but each time I could hear the blade coming. I could hear it inside my mind. I would move a little this way or that, but I remember times when the blade came to rest against my forehead."

After a silence the old soldier spoke again, "My trouble is that I can't forget that day. I can't forget it, and I can't forgive myself, and I can't forgive God. The years go by. I celebrate new anniversaries of the wound. I carve new pictures of it into my cane, but it never goes away. I believe that God betrayed me. I think he let the Russians see somehow that I was happy. I think it was God who tipped them off to come after me that Christmas Day."

"Ambushed by God?" Jean was silent for a moment. "That's worse than anything I've been through. Nowadays I mostly argue with the demon who lives in my chimney, but we are old comrades and quite evenly matched. In my youth it was only

Napoleon who was after me, and he seems to have given up after all. You won't believe this, but a few months back this new Napoleon of ours sent me a box. What could be in it?, I thought. Was it the long-delayed order for my execution? Even stranger, it was the Legion of Honor. I returned it with a note. I tried to explain that I am still a deserter. Even now I keep trying to desert. It's just that in my old age I am no longer lucky at it, so they keep recapturing me. The State may have forgotten all this, but I have not forgotten.

"While I was in the haystack, so lost and hidden beneath the mantle of the Virgin that Napoleon could not find me, the soldiers went to my father's house and took my brother François as my substitute." There was a rawness in his voice now and his eyes no longer met those of the old soldier. "We never found out exactly where he died. Germany, perhaps. If this new Napoleon wants to give out medals, he should find my brother and give the Legion of Honor to him."

This morning, Father Jean had decided to talk about Saint Joseph. The assistant priest handled all the masses now, but each morning, usually at an odd early lonely hour, Father Jean gave a little talk. That way all the penitents and pilgrims could at least see and hear him, even if they did not get a turn with him in the confessional. There was no longer time for the Father to do masses, not with all the confessions. Father Jean himself thought it was a hellish notion to go to confession with a priest who could read your thoughts. But people were like that. They never knew what was good for them. They came to confess to him in droves. Today, Christmas, it was a relief to see a few bona fide parishioners in the church, sitting there with all the tourists. They had come early to get a good seat for the Christmas mass that followed. The mayor was there, too. More and more the mayor followed Father Jean like a shadow, as if he could not get the old priest out of his mind.

In his talk Father Jean said that he thought we all worried too little about Saint Joseph. We all painted the birth of the

Christ in happy colors as if it were a perfectly wonderful day, a pure and glorious gift from God. Not so, from Joseph's point of view. His moment had come when Mary agreed to be his wife. After that it had been one shock after another: Mary pregnant by someone else. Romans ordering everyone home for tax collection. No room at the inn. No one to help with the birth. Nightmares. Shepherds, foreigners, and pilgrims crowding about all the time. Herod's soldiers coming to kill the baby. Fleeing as a refugee. It was not a good Christmas for Joseph. It had not even been a decent year for Joseph.

"So what is the meaning of all this for us today?" Father Jean always asked at the end of his little talks, even though he never came up with good answers. "Is our Christmas happiness so much different from Joseph's? Maybe we are imitating Mary's husband when we arrange our Christmas to be a series of shocks. We arrange to visit relatives in the dead of winter when the journey is most prone to catastrophe. We arrange to invite the boring neighbors whom we hate so we can labor for hours cooking delicacies they will not appreciate. The Protestants seem to believe that if one is miserable and desperate one has strayed from God's path. We know better. Saint Joseph teaches us that one can be at the exact center, the blinding focus of God's grace and love and still feel beleaguered by merciless shocks, disappointments, and frustrations."

Father Jean smiled, certain that everyone would be cheered by this vision (which somehow, paradoxically, they were). Then he bowed his head to pray. This, too, was something he did every day for a long time after his talk. Sometimes he would eavesdrop on people's thoughts and make comments back to them out loud. Comments like "Jeanette, just go ahead and marry the fellow. I would," or "George, no matter what you say, it is still a sin," or "Renée, why did you tell me such trivia in the confessional when you are carrying around this terrible secret like a ball of lead?" Jean would stand there making these comments more or less at random while various individuals would suddenly blush or wince or kneel or leave the church. Cynics and misanthropes felt this was the most pleasing part of the whole pilgrim show at Ars.

Today the audience would see something new, for as soon as Father Jean had started to pray the angel in the crèche behind him began whispering in his ear. "Your prayers have been answered, Father, through the intercession of Saint Joseph. This cross will be taken from you. Your mind will be healed. From now on you will no longer have to hear the thoughts of other people."

Father Jean said, "What do you mean? I asked for no more pilgrims and no more miraculous cures, not to stop hearing thoughts. I've gotten used to remembering other people's memories. I like that part now. It is most fascinating, really, a salve to my curiosity."

The angel looked exasperated. "This always happens when I try to answer a prayer. Never do I get a word of thanks. Instead I'm always sent back for revisions. Father, we have in our files over ten thousand of your prayers."

"Just make the pilgrims go away; that's what I want."

The angel shook her head. "Asking to be able to hear the thoughts of other people and not be treated like a freak is like asking to take a bath and not get wet. The Bureau of Natural Law would never allow it. They'd make a terrible fuss it we tried to do it that way. Natural Law told us there would be no problem at all about simply taking the gift away. All we have to do is arrange for another fever or a hard knock on the head. This last shouldn't be difficult at all to engineer since we have several hundred requests on file from the mayor to do just that. Natural Law has never quite forgiven us for putting that scar in your brain in the first place."

"That was an answer to a prayer, too?"

The angel nodded sternly. "This is why we in Heaven have to keep everything on file. In those days you were always bothering us for understanding. You wanted to know why people were cruel. You said you needed a way to stop judging everyone so harshly. You had no grasp on evil whatsoever. So we arranged it so you could hear other people's thoughts, and learn not to be shocked when they behaved badly."

"So that's why it happened."

"Well, of course. Not that we've ever heard any thanks at the time or since in my department," said the angel. "All we have heard are complaints, over ten thousand complaints in the recent past to be exact."

"I take them back. I rescind them one and all," said Father Jean. "Can't you transfer the favor though? There's a boy with a crutch sitting out there…"

"Do you imagine," asked the angel, "that he would welcome me any better than you have? No, thank you. We don't do transfers. No transfers, refunds, or exchanges. We can barely get answers to prayers accepted by the people who allegedly asked for the things themselves, much less try to rely on what some stranger imagines they really want. Wait until you are with us taking these orders, too, and trying to do your best, and what will you hear? Only complaints and self-pity."

Out in the congregation, the mayor saw Father gesturing and muttering to the angel and to Saint Joseph behind him in the crèche. "What's happened?" he asked the old captain and Philippe. "What's he doing now?"

"I think he's arguing with God," said the old soldier. That sounded right to the mayor. He thought he recognized the stubborn set of Father Jean's chin. It cheered the mayor up a little, too, because God didn't seem to be doing any better at arguing with Father Jean than the mayor had himself.

POSTSCRIPT

North Americans may not recognize the mischievous, anti-estab-lishment Mary to whom Jean Vianney surrendered. We have been taught to pray to a more straight-laced version of the Virgin, a Holy Mother dubbed by Garrison Keillor "Our Lady of Perpetual Respon-sibility." But Mary made her reputation in the Dark Ages as the last refuge against that submission to authority that authority defines as responsibility. The young knight quaking as he prayed before the battle would turn to find his armor gone. Mary had decided the test was too hard and had gone out to fight in his stead. Young nuns would pray that Mary replace them during the nightly bed checks while they sneaked out to meet their lovers. This sort of adventure has been Mary's specialty in Europe and especially France, leaving poor Saint Joseph and his male minions ever more at sea.

Jean Vianney finally gave up on running away and settled down to being a very good priest indeed. His demon weakened and wasted away but Father Jean never was able to sleep much. Next time you hear the song "Are You Sleeping Brother John?" (*Frère Jacques*), you'll know that the answer is no. In the last fifteen years of his life more than twenty thousand people visited Ars to confess to Jean Vianney. The old priest never ceased to rage and moan at this celebrity. He car-ried in his cassock handfuls of religious medals which he would throw to the pilgrims like Mardi Gras beads. Then while they were bent over picking them off the ground, Father Jean would dash away.

Jean Vianney is the patron saint of parish priests. He died August 4, 1859, and his day is celebrated on August 9.

Philomena was a teenage girl with a smashed skull whose bones were found in a Roman catacomb in the early years of the nine-teenth century. Hagiographers were dubious about her from the beginning and in 1961 her name was stricken from the calendar despite the many authenticated but inexplicable miracles attributed to her. Renegades who choose to celebrate Philomena regardless may do so on August 10. Jean Vianney got on well with her, I believe, because he was accustomed to having a woman at his side to take care of the heavy work and the unpleasant bits. It was the rectory housekeeper after all who supplied the muscle power in the epic battles with Jean's demon over the placement of the furniture. Before that, Jean had relied on his sister. While they watched sheep together, they were supposed to be making socks as well. Jean's sister would often find Jean's socks tossed into her lap with a breezy, over-the-shoulder, "You knit; I'll pray." Long-suffering sisters, wives, and daughters of such men might think of consulting Philomena. The Vatican may consider her a mistake, but somebody in the first century did bash in her head and she did put up with Jean Vianney for thirty years. All this experience has to count for something.

AND
ONE TO
SAVE
FOR
EASTER

JUDAS

THE MYSTERY OF
THE MISSING MATZOH

History never embraces more than a small part of reality.

—DUC FRANÇOIS DE LA ROCHEFOUCAULD

I affirm nothing. I only relate what I have heard
from people I found otherwise trustworthy,
but they may have deluded themselves in all sincerity.

—ALEXANDRIA DAVID-NEEL,
Magic and Mystery in Tibet

JUDAS

Easter has never been one of my favorite times. Take coloring the eggs. Remember how you would dip them into the glorious yellow, and then the bright bright red, and then the sky blue, trying to make a rainbow, but they always came out all purplish-brown. And you always burned your fingers boiling the eggs to begin with. Remember how even that debacle could not measure up to the horror of the Easter egg hunt itself, when cousin Andy, having swiftly secured every egg but one, was routinely thrashed into submission so that Little Jeanie could find that one? Which she usually could not, even given the advantage of a sullenly tethered Andy. Added to that festival unpleasantness there were the endless Lenten crucifixions of twice on Sunday and Wednesday services when hymn after hymn and call after call featured blood and thorns and whippings (mostly, I imagined, of cousin Andy) and Hell. I cannot believe the good Lord meant Easter to be that way. One has only to look at crocuses pushing stubbily up out of the snow to know that Easter was meant to be a time for celebrating some kind of magic. All this is why I have made up the following story, which seems, by some oversight to have been omitted from surviving versions of the New Testament.

THE MYSTERY OF THE
MISSING MATZOH

Passover is that time around Easter when people get together to feast and to remember how God helped the children of Israel escape from the wicked Pharoah.

A boiled egg is kept on the table during the feast. This is to remind everyone of how hot times make you tough inside, and also of how solid the Israelites became with each other after being burned a lot. There are bitter herbs to remind us of the bitterness of slavery and salt water so we can remember the tears, and greens to remind us of hope that stays its own budding self no matter what.

There are also matzohs at Passover. This is to remind everybody of how fast the Israelites had to leave Egypt; so fast that the only thing they had time to cook was so hard and tasteless it could scarcely be called bread.

Always, when the matzohs are blessed at the Passover meal, one piece is set aside to be hidden. This is to remind everyone of how hard it is to keep children from getting bored, even at Passover.

At the Last Supper it was Jesus who got to hide the matzoh. This was because He was the leader.

Everybody was in a pretty relaxed mood by then because they had just finished the second (or was it the third?) cup of wine. The apostles were there, of course, and Martha was there because she loved to cook a big meal for a crowd of people, and Luke because he hated to eat at the hospital.

Jesus was having a bit of fun with the matzoh before he hid it. He twirled it through His fingers and then spread it out into a deck of matzohs, but when He closed the deck there was only the one again.

Judas had come in late and was the only one of the twelve not rainbowed with Easter-egg dye. "Let's get this over with," he grumbled. "I don't see why we have to hide a matzoh at all this time. There aren't even children here tonight."

"Oh, Judas," said Jesus, looking around, "there are plenty of children here tonight. The only thing I despair of is finding a grown-up or two."

When Thomas (who had decided to make sure no one else was peeking) opened his eyes a brief microsecond later, there was no more matzoh, and Jesus, who was nonchalantly carving the lamb, gave him a big wink.

Then everyone began to feast and enjoy in earnest. It was a long laughing while until Jesus said it was time to search for the hidden matzoh. Peter was already under the table by then and everyone else was in similarly good position to begin the search.

John, who was naturally lucky, was the first to come up with something. Under his napkin he found a silver cup, the same battered cup with his fading name engraved on it, that he had been given for being born and had lost long ago. "What's this for?" he asked.

"It's for changes," said Jesus and, when John looked puzzled, tried to explain. "Poison to water, water to wine, wine to blood. Things like that. Changes."

Then Andrew found the fishhook he had invented when he was twelve, a cleverly carved X with a hook at each end. Andrew laughed because, for the first time after thousands of disappointing experiments, there was a fish attached to each of the four hooks.

Bartholemew found his first pocketknife under one of the plates, the knife his dad had bought for him at a fair. And James found the scallop shell he had kept in his treasure box all through his boyhood. When he put it to his ear, the sound took him right back to the sand and the sunset where he had first found that shell. Then the sea-song changed to something else, singing or words perhaps, or even screams and crackling flames, so James took it away from his ear and just held it for a while.

Everyone was finding childhood things that had been lost long ago. Matthew found his little hatchet and Philip his old hiking staff. Thaddeus found the carpenter's square he'd lost while building his brother's barn. Simon found his old fish-saw, and Jude his wolf-bashing club. Thomas found a gold piece from his old coin collection and kept biting on it to make sure it was real. Luke even found the stethoscope that had been stolen his third year of medical school.

Judas, who was always a bit nervous in the presence of fun, nearly jumped out of his skin when Jesus spoke to him. "What's that in your bag?" said Jesus. Judas looked down at the moneybag hanging from his neck and saw that it was wriggling and jumping and getting bigger.

"I don't know," said Judas, trying to straighten it out as if it were a tie. "I don't know and you don't want to know." But the bag kept right on jumping until something started writhing and leaping and pushing its way out of it. When the something emerged, it was a huge amber-eyed, witch-bred black cat.

Jesus clucked his tongue. "I think you have already let the cat out of the bag?"

Judas's eyes began to shift and his hand trembled so that he spilled wine all over his beautiful white robe. Jesus smiled and pointed to his own robe which was besplattered and besmirched with Easter-egg dye. "The Man is becoming more lunatic each day," thought Judas. "I'm getting out just in time."

"A few more mistakes like that," said Jesus, "and you could

begin to fit right in here." But Judas just shook his fist, muttering something about clumsy oafs, and sent Martha out for peroxide. Jesus sighed. "The only thing that shocks me about you—aside from the fact that you did not ask a higher price—(Jesus shook his head sadly at Judas's moneybag) is that you have not yet shed a single tear. I suppose righteous indignation carries one through. But it would make me feel infinitely better about the whole thing if you would weep just one tear. For old times' sake."

Judas fixed his eyes on a point several inches above Christ's head and tried to look as if he didn't understand a word.

Suddenly, Jesus snapped his fingers. "I've got it. One parting magic trick for you, my friend Judas." The latter winced. He hated to see the Master stoop to such childishness and base carnival frippery. Jesus laughed and, pulling a wand from his sleeve, waved it in the direction of Judas's left ear.

Suddenly a rather shaggy white rabbit popped out of that ear and made directly for Judas's nose, shedding all the way. Judas turned all pale and sneezed so hard he blew the rabbit halfway across the room. "You see," said Jesus, "I've been trying to remember what it is that you are allergic to. It wasn't cats; it was rabbits." Jesus continued to make free with his wand, and a second rabbit popped out of Judas's right ear, then another from the left, and so forth until Judas's eyes were red and streaming and the room was full of happy hopping rabbits.

"Ah," said Jesus. "That feels much better." Then He pulled a string of many-colored bandanas out of his sleeve and gave them to Judas. "Blow your nose and go," He said, a bit too hastily to be entirely polite. And so Jesus ushered Judas and several score of white rabbits to the door.

Jesus seemed suddenly quite gay. "Where is Peter?" He asked, peering under the tablecloth. "Time to get this party going." At that moment a cock crowed loudly.

"Is it you Charley?" beamed Peter, fumbling in his shirt. He pulled out a gleaming, strutting, red-and-black rooster. "It's

Charley! I thought I would not see you again, my friend," Peter chuckled as he patted the rooster's comb.

That rooster had been part of Peter's first double life. Long ago, he had "borrowed" that cock from his master every evening and made the rounds of the cockfights. The arrangement fell apart one night when Peter, on his way home from the cockfights, ran into his master on the road. "Where have you been?" he asked. "Out swimming," said Peter, knowing even as he said it that his lips were trembling and his ears were red and his hair was not wet. At that point the rooster crowed from beneath his shirt and that game ended. "So must this double life end, too," thought Peter, wondering if he would ever have the courage to tell his granny what he was really doing. She thought he was working as an altar boy for a very respectable and aged Orthodox rabbi.

"Back to business," said Jesus. "I believe, gentlemen, that we were looking for a missing matzoh."

The besotted group came approximately to order.

"And look," said Jesus, "here it is right now right in front of us in the beak of Peter's pet cock." So saying, Jesus pulled the matzoh out of the rooster's mouth, blessed it and broke it and gave it to His disciples.

POSTSCRIPT

The rest of the story you know. The missing matzoh is only the tiniest piece of that particularly vast and ongoing jigsaw puzzle. Even so, the story contains a few small answers to those very small questions that most bedevil and bother children.

"What does the Easter Rabbit have to do with Jesus?" the children ask. Now you can see that we honor the Rabbit at Easter because it was Rabbit who brought old Judas to tears if not to repentance. Old Rabbit got through to Judas's poor allergic eyes when even Jesus could not touch that traitor's hard and self-righteous heart. Why, you may ask, is Saint John always painted holding a cup, Saint Andrew holding an X, James with a shell, and so forth? It is because these are the things they found on that famous matzoh hunt. And each time we hunt Easter eggs there is always the hope that we, too, may discover some special magic that will help us make sense of our own past and future.

"Why do we color the Easter eggs?" ask the children. We boil the poor eggs until we are sure they're dead and then we make the eggs bright and gay with colors, so that they dye a second time. This is because Jesus showed us there is joy to be had even in being boiled if it is done for and with one's friends.

Why do we get bright-colored new clothes at Easter? This is because the disciples made such a mess of dyeing eggs that first Easter that they turned their clothes into rainbows. So at Easter-time we try, in deed and in dress, to turn the mess that each of us truly is into a rainbow.

REFERENCES

If, as you have read about these saints, you have tried to look up any of them in the encyclopedia or at the library, you will have noticed that not only are my stories fiction but also my history is some combination of guess, gosh, and arbitrary side-taking about imaginary answers to unknowable questions. This is true for even the most trivial of hoped-for facts like the dates these people lived or the days on which we celebrate them (the latter keep getting shifted around by the Church as it rearranges its calendar to make room for ever-more new saints). Should you care to enter this scholarly fray and discover the real stories and the true answers, the following books would be places to start.

Bataille, Georges. *The Trial of Gilles de Rais: Documents Presented by Georges Bataille*. Los Angeles: Amok, 1991. (Originally published in France.)

DeNevi, Don, and Noel Frances Moholy. *Junípero Serra*. New York: Harper & Row, 1985.

Devlin, Christopher. *The Life of Robert Southwell, Poet and Martyr*. New York: Farrar, Straus, and Cudahy, 1956.

Erikson, Joan Mowat. *Saint Francis and His Four Ladies*. New York: Norton, 1981.

Gerard, John. Edited by John Morris. *The Conditions of Catholics under James I: Father Gerard's Narrative of the Gunpowder Plot*. London: Longmans Green, 1871.

Merton, Thomas (translator). *The Wisdom of the Desert: Sayings from the Desert Fathers of the Fourth Century*. New York: New Directions, 1960.

Nicholl, Charles. *The Reckoning*. London: Johnathan Cape, 1992.

Thurston, H.J., and D. Attwater. *Butler's Lives of the Saints*. Complete edition. Four volumes. Westminster, MD: Christian Classics, 1981.

Trochu, Abbé Francis. *The Curé d'Ars: St. Jean Marie Baptiste Vianney*. Rockford, IL: TAN, 1977.

Warner, Marina. *Joan of Arc: The Image of Female Heroism*. Middlesex, Eng.: Penguin Books, 1983. (Originally published in France.)